T3-AJJ-957

Praise for *In Your Face*

"*In Your Face* by Johny Johansson should be required reading for every American student of business. The book shows the difference between American, Japanese and European marketing. And it explains why American marketing is stirring up Anti-Americanism in foreign countries. Thus, the book not only helps the international marketer to take such 'side-effects' into consideration when deciding on the optimal balance between localization and standardization. More importantly, the book raises the question of the American manager's societal responsibilities. *In Your Face* is a very personal, very engaging statement by a truly international academic. It is thought-provoking and should stimulate a much-needed debate on America's role in the world."

—Gert Assmus, Professor Emeritus at the Amos Tuck School, Dartmouth College, former Dean at Leipzig Graduate School of Management

"Johansson combines insightful global vision and rigorous analytical skills in framing the many complex global issues facing American firms and brands. *In Your Face* is an honest, thoughtful, and provocative essay on 'brand America' and the good, bad, and ugly of American marketing practices globally."

—Gary Bamossy, Director, Global Business Program, University of Utah, Professor of Marketing, Vrije Universiteit, Amsterdam, and co-author of *Consumer Behaviour: A European Perspective*

"When a leading marketing theorist explains why U.S. marketing tactics spark big blowbacks for U.S. products and its global reputation, we had all better listen. In this book, Johansson connects the unconnectable: the in-your-face marketing style of U.S. advertisers and the ongoing cultural/political decline of the U.S. image in world affairs. A fan of Johny Johansson's work for years, I find this his most potent contribution to date."

—Thomas Donaldson, Mark O. Winkelman Professor, The Wharton School, University of Pennsylvania, and author of *The Ethics of International Business*

"Johansson develops a controversial idea: Efforts by U.S.-based firms to create overseas brand recognition often fan anti-American feelings even where the brands themselves become commercial successes. This makes for reading that is both highly provocative and entertaining, especially recommended for anyone who seeks to understand the paradox of why, in so many countries, local residents who dislike America nonetheless want to hang out at Starbucks."

—Edward M. Graham, Senior Fellow, Institute for International Economics, Washington, D.C., and author of *Fighting the Wrong Enemy: Antiglobalist Activists and Multinational Enterprises*

"In view of the wide-spread discontent with marketing and marketing practices, especially among the young all across the globe, this book is right to the point. Johny K. Johansson, himself a prominent marketing scholar, expresses his own deep concern with the negative aspects of today's marketing practices, and gives ideas about remedies for this state of affairs. Although one may disagree with some of his ideas, the book gives an important starting point for a discussion of the consequences of 'unlimited' marketing, a discussion that is long overdue among established politicians, policy makers and media. Needless to say, this book, used in marketing classes, will spark lively and fiery discussions about the consequences of marketing and of the importance of the development of more balanced marketing practicies than, according to Johansson's thought-provoking book, are at hand today."

—Claes-Robert Julander, Ragnar Söderberg Professor of Business
Administration, Stockholm School of Economics

"Every major force in society—religion, technology, marketing—has its dark side. Johny Johansson, a prominent marketing academic, confesses to the darker side of American marketing practice as it manifests itself in Hummers, obesity, disrespect for the consumer, environmental degradation, feeding of greed and lust, junk mail and phone calls, commercialism, and insensitivity to local cultures and needs. Johansson shows how competitive pressure and marketing's brashness have contributed to anti-marketing, anti-globalism, and anti-Americanism. He spells out the ambivalence felt by many marketers about the impact of their craft on the quality of life around the world. You may not agree with all of his conclusions, but he has eloquently expressed his deep concern about the commercialized consumption culture created by American marketing. This book should be read by marketers, senior managers, and public policy people to stimulate fresh debate about how to rebalance marketing so that it produces fewer 'bads.'"

—Philip Kotler, Distinguished Professor of International Marketing,
The Kellogg School of Management,
and author of *Marketing Management*, 11th edition

"Prof. Johansson has provided us with a penetrating analysis of the role of global marketing and the causes of hostility to it, an analysis from the perspective of an insider and an expert. While he is no cheerleader for the global justice movement, he takes its many elements seriously and tries to arrive at an intellectually rigorous and morally informed evaluation of global marketing. The result is a book that should be of great value to anyone interested in the effects of globalization, whatever their antecedent opinions."

—Mark Lance, Associate Professor, Philosophy Department,
Georgetown University

"Nobody else than Johny Johansson could better demonstrate the combined impact on public opinion of three major social change drivers: Marketing, Globalization, and Americanism. But in addition, Johny Johansson helps us in separating good and bad practices. A must-read for every global marketeer!"

— **Prof. Jean-Claude Larreche, Alfred H. Heineken Chair of Marketing, INSEAD, and co-author of *Marketing Strategy*, 4th edition**

"*In Your Face* shows great insight in describing how in many areas of social, political, commercial and economic activity, American single-mindedness can distort reality and blindside decision makers. Johansson demonstrates for example that a heavy focus on market goals to the exclusion of wider considerations can nurture anti-globalization, anti-Americanism and a negative attitude towards free trade and open markets. The book's international scope ensures that it has potential readership overseas as well as in America. In an era of intense global competition and a reluctance to compromise, *In Your Face* serves as a useful antidote and should be widely read by market researchers, business executives and policy planners generally. I found this book stimulating and relevant to our time. I trust that it will enjoy the wide readership that it deserves."

— **Owen Price, Development Economist (ret.), The World Bank, former Head of the Iran mission**

"Johansson's brilliant book should thrill any intelligent and free mind: He challenges us to think about our personal lives and our marketing profession, and on what does global marketing really contribute and how does it fit in this 21st century post-modern world."

— **Prof. Lluís G. Renart, Ph.D., IESE Business School, Universidad de Navarra, Spain**

"What a treat, and what a surprise! A welcome critique of marketing, especially the American 'in your face' variety, from within the marketing field. It is readable, accessible, enjoyable, informative and sometimes infuriating. The reader never need guess where Johansson stands and most often feels the need to stand there with him. A revealing discussion of the role of marketing and branding in Americanization and globalization as well as the anti-Americanism and anti-globalization movements that seem to be their frequent companions. Covered are many brands, countries and a wide range of issues. In the process, the 'in your face' critique is extended in a number of directions (the marketing of religion, for example), including to the current Bush administration and its largely unsuccessful efforts to market aggressively (given the President's MBA) the 2003 war in Iraq. A great read anywhere, including while you're eating your Big Mac or drinking your vente coffee at Starbucks, although be forewarned—the text might force you to want to leave before you finish."

— **George Ritzer, Distinguished University Professor, The University of Maryland, and author of *The McDonaldization of Society***

"The book is a real gem: full of interesting examples and personal observations, it goes beyond the usual bold critique of marketing, globalization and U.S. dominance to deliver a sensible vision of hope that does not throw out the baby with the bathwater."

—Professor Bodo B. Schlegelmilch, Ph.D., Chair of International Marketing and Management, Academic Director of Vienna Executive MBA, Vienna University of Economics and Business Administration

"This book offers a very thoughtful and passionate wakeup call to all of us who believe in the American way to global marketing. Johny Johansson convincingly argues that American marketing successes in the global market place are like a potent drug: the cure is worse than the illness. If you practice marketing, you must read this book even though it will make you uncomfortable."

—Jagdish N. Sheth, Charles H. Kellstadt Professor of Marketing, Goizueta Business School, Emory University

"This book, by a leading authority on global marketing, is a damning indictment of modern marketing from one of its own. Professor Johansson's thesis is that American marketing has always been 'in your face,' but never with the ubiquity and volume found today. But he doesn't stop there, as he develops his argument to show that these marketing practices have contributed substantially to both anti-Americanism and anti-globalization. He goes further still as he turns his attention to the use of similar techniques by the Bush White House before concluding with a vision of a more mature consumer culture. With its breadth of scope and rich mix of scholarly analysis and more personal reflections, this highly readable book should not only be required reading for marketers—however uncomfortable it might be—but also recommended to thoughtful consumers trying to figure out why spending more is inversely related to their quality of life."

—N. Craig Smith, Associate Professor of Marketing and Ethics, and Associate Dean of the Full-Time MBA Programme, London Business School, U.K., and co-author of *Ethics in Marketing*

"Global brand managers seek to push individuals out of friendship, citizenship, and culture spaces into a standardized 'consumerspace' with aggressive 'in your face' marketing. Johny Johansson argues that these practices of U.S. multinationals have evoked a reaction that is anti-capitalist, anti-American, and anti-consumerism. He persuasively calls for marketers to balance their focus on global branding with a renewed sensitivity to local and national cultures. Only in this way can the attack of anti-globalization forces be defended against. Johansson's compelling message is that global marketing is often bad marketing. It foists unneeded and inappropriate products on emerging societies in ways that stir resentment—and it has to change. Marketing managers everywhere should read this book."

—Jeremiah Sullivan, Ph.D., Professor at School of Business, University of Washington, and author of *The Future of Corporate Globalization*

In Your Face

How American Marketing Excess Fuels Anti-Americanism

Johny K. Johansson

An Imprint of PEARSON EDUCATION
Upper Saddle River, NJ • New York • London • San Francisco • Toronto • Sydney
Tokyo • Singapore • Hong Kong • Cape Town • Madrid
Paris • Milan • Munich • Amsterdam

www.ft-ph.com

Library of Congress Cataloging-in-Publication Data

Johansson, Johny K.
  In your face : how American marketing excess fuels anti-Americanism / by Johny K.
Johansson
    p. cm.
  Includes index.
  ISBN 0-13-143818-2
    1. Export marketing--Political aspects--United States. 2. Export marketing--Moral and ethical
  aspects--United States. 3. Advertising--Moral and ethical aspects--United States. 4. Anti-
  Americanism. I. Title.
HF1416.J634 2004
303.48'273--dc22   2003064361

Editorial/Production Supervision: *Donna Cullen-Dolce*
Developmental Editor: *Russ Hall*
Cover Design Director: *Jerry Votta*
Cover Design: *Mary Jo DeFranco*
Art Director: *Gail Cocker-Bogusz*
Manufacturing Buyer: *Maura Zaldivar*
VP, Editor-in-Chief: *Tim Moore*
Marketing Manager: *John Pierce*
Editorial Assistant: *Richard Winkler*

 © 2004 Pearson Education, Inc.
Publishing as Financial Times Prentice Hall
Upper Saddle River, New Jersey 07458

Financial Times Prentice Hall offers excellent discounts on this book when ordered in
quantity for bulk purchases or special sales. For more information, please contact: U.S.
Corporate and Government Sales, 1-800-382-3419, corpsales@pearsontechgroup.com.
For sales outside of the U.S., please contact: International Sales, 1-317-581-3793,
international@pearsontechgroup.com.

1st Printing
ISBN 0-13-143818-2

Pearson Education Ltd.
Pearson Education Australia Pty, Limited
Pearson Education Singapore, Pte. Ltd.
Pearson Education North Asia Ltd.
Pearson Education Canada, Ltd.
Pearson Educación de Mexico, S.A. de C.V.
Pearson Education—Japan
Pearson Education Malaysia, Pte. Ltd

for
Anna and Sonja

FT Prentice Hall

FINANCIAL TIMES

In an increasingly competitive world, it is quality
of thinking that gives an edge—an idea that opens new
doors, a technique that solves a problem, or an insight
that simply helps make sense of it all.

We work with leading authors in the various arenas
of business and finance to bring cutting-edge thinking
and best learning practice to a global market.

It is our goal to create world-class print publications
and electronic products that give readers
knowledge and understanding which can then be
applied, whether studying or at work.

To find out more about our business
products, you can visit us at www.ft-ph.com

Pearson
Education

FINANCIAL TIMES PRENTICE HALL BOOKS

For more information, please go to www.ft-ph.com

Business and Society

Douglas K. Smith
> *On Value and Values: Thinking Differently About We in an Age of Me*

Business and Technology

Sarv Devaraj and Rajiv Kohli
> *The IT Payoff: Measuring the Business Value of Information Technology Investments*

Nicholas D. Evans
> *Business Innovation and Disruptive Technology: Harnessing the Power of Breakthrough Technology...for Competitive Advantage*

Nicholas D. Evans
> *Consumer Gadgets: 50 Ways to Have Fun and Simplify Your Life with Today's Technology...and Tomorrow's*

Faisal Hoque
> *The Alignment Effect: How to Get Real Business Value Out of Technology*

Economics

David Dranove
> *What's Your Life Worth? Health Care Rationing...Who Lives? Who Dies? Who Decides?*

John C. Edmunds
> *Brave New Wealthy World: Winning the Struggle for World Prosperity*

Jonathan Wight
> *Saving Adam Smith: A Tale of Wealth, Transformation, and Virtue*

Entrepreneurship

Oren Fuerst and Uri Geiger
> *From Concept to Wall Street: A Complete Guide to Entrepreneurship and Venture Capital*

David Gladstone and Laura Gladstone
> *Venture Capital Handbook: An Entrepreneur's Guide to Raising Venture Capital, Revised and Updated*

Thomas K. McKnight
> *Will It Fly? How to Know if Your New Business Idea Has Wings... Before You Take the Leap*

Erica Orloff and Kathy Levinson, Ph.D.
> *The 60-Second Commute: A Guide to Your 24/7 Home Office Life*

Jeff Saperstein and Daniel Rouach
> *Creating Regional Wealth in the Innovation Economy: Models, Perspectives, and Best Practices*

Stephen Spinelli, Jr., Robert M. Rosenberg, and Sue Birley
> *Franchising: Pathway to Wealth Creation*

Executive Skills

Cyndi Maxey and Jill Bremer
  It's Your Move: Dealing Yourself the Best Cards in Life and Work

Finance

Aswath Damodaran
  The Dark Side of Valuation: Valuing Old Tech, New Tech, and New Economy Companies

Kenneth R. Ferris and Barbara S. Pécherot Petitt
  Valuation: Avoiding the Winner's Curse

International Business and Globalization

Johny K. Johansson
  In Your Face: How American Marketing Excess Fuels Anti-Americanism

Peter Marber
  Money Changes Everything: How Global Prosperity Is Reshaping Our Needs, Values, and Lifestyles

Fernando Robles, Françoise Simon, and Jerry Haar
  Winning Strategies for the New Latin Markets

Investments

Zvi Bodie and Michael J. Clowes
  Worry-Free Investing: A Safe Approach to Achieving Your Lifetime Goals

Aswath Damodaran
  Investment Fables: Exposing the Myths of "Can't Miss" Investment Strategies

Harry Domash
  Fire Your Stock Analyst! Analyzing Stocks on Your Own

David Gladstone and Laura Gladstone
  Venture Capital Investing: The Complete Handbook for Investing in Businesses for Outstanding Profits

D. Quinn Mills
  Buy, Lie, and Sell High: How Investors Lost Out on Enron and the Internet Bubble

D. Quinn Mills
  Wheel, Deal, and Steal: Deceptive Accounting, Deceitful CEOs, and Ineffective Reforms

John Nofsinger and Kenneth Kim
  Infectious Greed: Restoring Confidence in America's Companies

John R. Nofsinger
  Investment Blunders (of the Rich and Famous)…And What You Can Learn from Them

John R. Nofsinger
  Investment Madness: How Psychology Affects Your Investing…And What to Do About It

H. David Sherman, S. David Young, and Harris Collingwood
  Profits You Can Trust: Spotting & Surviving Accounting Landmines

Leadership

Jim Despain and Jane Bodman Converse
  And Dignity for All: Unlocking Greatness through Values-Based Leadership

Marshall Goldsmith, Vijay Govindarajan, Beverly Kaye, and Albert A. Vicere
  The Many Facets of Leadership

Marshall Goldsmith, Cathy Greenberg, Alastair Robertson, and Maya Hu-Chan
  Global Leadership: The Next Generation

Management

Rob Austin and Lee Devin
  Artful Making: What Managers Need to Know About How Artists Work

J. Stewart Black and Hal B. Gregersen
  Leading Strategic Change: Breaking Through the Brain Barrier

William C. Byham, Audrey B. Smith, and Matthew J. Paese
  Grow Your Own Leaders: How to Identify, Develop, and Retain Leadership Talent

David M. Carter and Darren Rovell
  On the Ball: What You Can Learn About Business from Sports Leaders

Subir Chowdhury
  Organization 21C: Someday All Organizations Will Lead this Way

Ross Dawson
  *Living Networks: Leading Your Company, Customers, and Partners
  in the Hyper-connected Economy*

Charles J. Fombrun and Cees B.M. Van Riel
  Fame and Fortune: How Successful Companies Build Winning Reputations

Amir Hartman
  Ruthless Execution: What Business Leaders Do When Their Companies Hit the Wall

Harvey A. Hornstein
  *The Haves and the Have Nots: The Abuse of Power and Privilege in the Workplace…
  and How to Control It*

Kevin Kennedy and Mary Moore
  Going the Distance: Why Some Companies Dominate and Others Fail

Roy H. Lubit
  Coping with Toxic Managers, Subordinates…and Other Difficult People

Robin Miller
  The Online Rules of Successful Companies: The Fool-Proof Guide to Building Profits

Fergus O'Connell
  The Competitive Advantage of Common Sense: Using the Power You Already Have

Tom Osenton
  The Death of Demand: The Search for Growth in a Saturated Global Economy

W. Alan Randolph and Barry Z. Posner
  *Checkered Flag Projects: 10 Rules for Creating and Managing Projects that Win,
  Second Edition*

Stephen P. Robbins
  Decide & Conquer: Make Winning Decisions to Take Control of Your Life

Stephen P. Robbins
  The Truth About Managing People…And Nothing but the Truth

Ronald Snee and Roger Hoerl
  *Leading Six Sigma: A Step-by-Step Guide Based on Experience with GE and Other
  Six Sigma Companies*

Contents

ACKNOWLEDGMENTS

I have discussed the topics in this book with a number of people in a number of places: at workshops, seminars, and conferences; in the classroom and over the Internet; at lunches, dinners, and over the phone; with relatives and neighbors, professionals, and experts; and with friends who agree with me and friends who disagree strongly. It's been a tough couple of years for my wife and two daughters, who would rather focus on their own lives than discuss the latest negative news. My only excuse is that they were the ones who got me started on the book in the first place, and that these have been difficult years for a lot of people in a lot of places, including our friends in Tokyo, my wife's hometown.

Among Washington friends, I would like to mention Monty Graham at the Institute of International Economics with his pro-trade views; Owen Price and George Zaidan both with useful World Bank experience and perspectives on Islam; Emily Price with State Department viewpoints; David Ashley of the Department of Homeland Security; Terry Gerace of the Toxic-Tobacco Law Coalition; my Georgetown University colleagues Dennis Quinn, Mike Ryan, George Brenkert, as well as Michael Czinkota, a true conservative; and Mark Lance in the Philosophy Department at Georgetown, a true anarchist. In the marketing world, I would like to thank my colleagues at Georgetown, Alan Andreasen, Ronnie Goodstein, and Marlene Morris; Philip Kotler at Northwestern; Case Julander at Stockholm School of Economics; Gerald Zaltman at Harvard; and Mike Mazis at American University. Ilkka Ronkainen and Ken Homa and the Landor organization were helpful with the branding analysis developed in the book, but I know they disagree with my negative take on some branding strategies. Amitabh Mungale provided many worthwhile viewpoints, as did Jerry Sullivan at the University of Washington in Seattle, Alan Rugman at Indiana, and Lluis Renart at IESE Barcelona. I owe special thanks to Gary Bamossy at Utah, whose perspective on Europe seen through an American expatriate's eyes was very useful and inspiring. Chuck Weinberg and his colleagues at the University of British Columbia in Vancouver showed how strongly some of these issues are felt in Canada. In Sweden, several of my old friends from the Stockholm School of Economics offered suggestions, including Lasse Bostrom, Goran Wiklund, and Lars Olofsson. So did Jan Segerfeldt, Hans Traugott, Amanda Haworth-Wiklund, and Per Johansson, my nephew who travels the globe for Dyno-Nobel, the dynamite company. Tak Sonoda of Honda, my colleague Masaaki Hirano at Waseda University, and my former students Yumi Goto and Mitch Murata offered sometimes widely different but still useful assessments of the Japanese perceptions and attitudes, as did, of course, my own in-house expert. Thanks to global technology, my wife can now watch the NHK television channel in real time and receive the Asahi Shimbun newspaper when her parents do.

My assistants Cipriano De Leon, Rushabh Doshi, and Jennifer Barker were resourceful not only in finding sources and data, but also in helping to develop the ideas expressed in the book. Cipriano also used his MBA alumni network around the world to collect information about perceptions from various countries, including Reza Moshir-Fatemi in London, Sean Nakamura in Munich, Ian Fuchsloch in Sao Paolo, and Sinan Akkaya in Istanbul. A special thank you goes to Tim Moore, my editor, Donna Cullen-Dolce, my production editor, and to Russ Hall, whose insightful and timely comments guided the project from start to finish. Russ deserves a lot of credit for challenging me to clarify the ideas and viewpoints expressed. So does David Arnold, whose European perspective was very helpful, and Rajeev Batra at the University of Michigan.

To all these people I am very grateful. Needless to say, they should be absolved of responsibility for the ideas expressed here. I just hope they agree with enough of the book to find it enjoyable—and also that the next few years will be an improvement on what the new millennium has brought so far.

Washington, D.C.—October 2003

PREFACE

This book started as an investigation into the complaints against marketing in the anti-globalization movement at the beginning of the new millennium. Not only did anti-globalizers attack sweatshop practices, child labor, and environmental degradation in third-world countries, they also denigrated the global brands I used as examples of good global marketing in my Master's of Business Administration (MBA) courses. Books appeared deploring the "McDonaldization" of society, and self-proclaimed anti-marketers advocated the boycott of leading brands. Young teenagers, including my own two daughters, refused to buy leading brands carefully targeted to them using our most advanced marketing techniques.

My daughters made me think. While I was touting Nike in class as a great example of global outsourcing and brand building, my own daughters participated in anti-globalization demonstrations against the brand. Starbucks, the globalizing chain of coffee houses, was picketed because their strategy of blanketing neighborhoods with Starbucks outlets forced local cafes out of business. The Gap, Disney, and McDonald's, iconic brands for us in marketing, were disparaged, or "dissed," in chat rooms on the Web. This needed some explanation.

After I started to write, the anti-globalization movement gradually morphed into another kind of movement. You all know what happened. On September 11, 2001, terrorists attacked the World Trade Center and the Pentagon. It was sort of anti-globalization gone berserk. As people around the world voiced support for the

Americans, the air seemed to have gone out of the anti-globalization movement. This was way bigger than just international trade or economics. I put the preliminary draft on the shelf for the time being.

But as America turned the war on terrorism into a war on Iraq, and in the process lost the support of its allies, the anti-globalization movement turned first into an anti-war movement, and then into an anti-American movement abroad. And now marketing issues seemed relevant again. For one thing, the rhetorical style of the Bush administration's war campaign very much resembled the in-your-face communication strategies common in American marketing. In addition, the unilateral war talk removed any foreign inhibitions against attacking America and its brands, reawakening the animosity toward globalization. The Americans were the main proponents of war, and they were also the main proponents of globalization. Anti-Americanism and anti-globalization seemed two sides of the same coin, and marketing surely played a common role in both movements. Exploring this role seemed important. I got back to the book. This is the result.

1 THREE STRIKES

No joy in Mudville...

I don't know how you feel, but in the past couple of years, a number of things have happened that make me feel as if the world is crumbling. I don't refer specifically to 9/11, although that is part of it. I am not really thinking of the Enron and Worldcom scandals or the dot-com crash either, although in some ways, they are also part of it. I am thinking of things that have happened both before and after 9/11.

I teach marketing and international business at Georgetown University in Washington, D.C.—according to the new Department of Homeland Security, nowadays one of the most dangerous places in the U.S. My specialty is global marketing. In the name of "full disclosure," I used to be a confirmed pro-globalizer, believing in the essential goodness of free trade and open access to foreign markets. I still do, to some extent. But we market globalizers have taken some hits recently, not only from 9/11, but also from usually benign sources.

You could say that I have had three slaps in my face. Anti-marketing campaigns by people I respected was the first blow, one that began in the earnest toward the end of the 1990s. Adbusters, affluenza, energy waste, fattest people on earth, and other headlines attacked marketing as the purveyor of filth and sloth, not customer satisfaction, as our questionnaires recorded.

Then came anti-globalization and Naomi Klein's No Logo, attacking predatory free trade and the dominance of global brands. I thought global marketers were bringing good things to people. Third came the anti-Americanism abroad, fueled by political invective that went counter to all the international sensitivity we taught in the business school. I call these slaps the "three strikes"—the baseball call that you've struck out.

Yes, my world has certainly changed from when I first started my career. I liked marketing, I liked globalization, and I liked America. I don't know how you feel, but I am going to fight this lowdown feeling of mine. Things can't be all that bad, can they?

Strike One: Anti-Marketing

I am looking at a flyer that came in the mail. It's an advertisement for the Hummer H1, the wide-bodied, high-riding military vehicle from General Motors, adapted for roadway driving. The written copy is personalized:

"Dear Mr. Johansson. There's a certain feeling that goes along with power. It's a compulsion that brings together the elements of respect, admiration, and yes, fear. And there's only one vehicle on the road today that delivers true power: HUMMER H1.

"Parker's HUMMER invites you to experience this incredible aphrodisiac... We think you'll agree: Power can be very, very addictive."

This kind of stuff makes me cringe. I am not a queasy person; I don't mind a bit of intimidation now and then. Heck, I played ice hockey and lost my front teeth as a teenager, and I tried to bluff my way through Checkpoint Charlie when the Berlin Wall was far from gone. I teach my kids when they drive to point the car so as to leave other drivers in no doubt about the direction in which they are going, and to make sure to take their turn (or better) at stop signs. But this was "over and above." Why, the Hummer is not simply an obvious step or two beyond the sport-utility vehicles (SUVs)—it's literally a threat to other drivers. And that, my flyer suggested, is its main attraction.

I have a doctorate in marketing from the University of California at Berkeley. I teach marketing to Master of Business Administration (MBA) students and undergraduates, plus the occasional executive. But it does not take a marketing degree to decipher this stuff. The Hummer—according to newspapers now one of the most popular large, luxury SUVs, and one of the most successful car introductions in the U.S. ever—appeals to the animalistic desire for dominance, sexual prowess, and sheer hedonistic pleasure in people.[1] And these drives are not simply male prerogatives anymore—at least not in the U.S. As casual observation and reports show, a significant percentage of SUV drivers are women, and newer SUVs seem to be the preferred mode of transportation for many of the once weaker sex as well. Another tally mark for the French and their "Vive la différence!"

According to a report by Morley Shafer on the CBS television (TV) program *60 Minutes* (broadcast on March 2, 2003), American automakers go to expensive consultants and conduct extensive market research to figure out why people want an SUV or a Hummer. Although I don't really want to bite the hand that feeds me, I must confess I find the resources spent rather misguided. It does not take much mental effort to understand these basic drives.[2] The question is whether people should be encouraged through advertising and these kinds of products to indulge their lowest level, instinctual cravings. And, if you really want to be a professional marketer in this mold, why not use some imagination and do a co-branding campaign featuring Hummer H1 and Viagra? There's no need to research that one, for after all, the target customers for the Hummer are not necessarily the men and

1. It also got a boost from the war in Iraq. According to Cristina Rouvalis, *Pittsburgh Post-Gazette,* April 23, 2003, p. E1, people flash thumbs-up signs at the civilian cousins of the Humvees they see on TV traversing the sand in Iraq. "It's a very patriotic vehicle," says Duane Guthrie, product manager at Wright Hummer in Wexford. "Some of my customers are talking about being patriotic."

2. Keith Bradsher's *High and Mighty: SUVs: The World's Most Dangerous Vehicles and How They Got That Way* (Public Affairs), 2002, offers an interesting discussion of the psychology behind SUVs, especially in Chapter 6, "Reptile Dreams."

women looking to power up their road-rage arsenal, they could also be aged people with doubts about their vitality and a willingness to spend some discretionary income to shore up their sagging confidence. At least that was, I figured, how the Hummer people found me when scrolling through their marketing database.

The marketing threat

Actually, I was glad the Hummer marketer did not simply call me on the phone. Junk mail is less intrusive and annoying than those telemarketing calls at dinnertime—well, not only at dinnertime, as it turns out. Now that I frequently work at home, I have found out that the calls start at 9 in the morning—8 a.m. on Saturdays—and continue throughout the day at hourly intervals. I know this is similar for other people, since I make sure that the talk around the water cooler when I'm in the office explores new devices to stop these calls. For a Christmas gift, my assistant gave me a TeleZapper, which promised to erase my phone number from any computer-assisted call list within two seconds after the first ring, provided I did not speak into the mouthpiece. The problem was that the laser-like beeping designed to incapacitate the computer mainly served to pierce the eardrums of everyone on the line. Whether or not it had any effect on the computer was never clear since the calls kept coming; it did, however, incapacitate one device: our cordless phone unit.

So, I have had to disconnect the TeleZapper, and have gone back to my original strategy. It consists of quickly answering "Hello" when picking up and hanging up within 1–2 seconds if nobody comes on the line. It usually takes a second or so for the telemarketer to get on the line, and even if he or she does get on quickly, the misread "Mr. Jonassen" or cheerful "Mr. Johnson" is enough of a giveaway to justify rejection. The key is never to get into that upsetting conversation that privacy advocates so rightly worry about. And don't worry about the telemarketer calling back right away; the computer keeps him or her moving to another number in short order. The only ones who will call back are the people you want to talk to, and they will be quicker to speak the second time. I have also, of course, recorded our phone numbers with the new DoNotCall.com registry, but plan to keep practicing this tried and true strategy. Given past experiences and the telemarketers' ingenuity, I am not sure how effective such a registry will be.

Yes, we in marketing have surely helped create a society that requires a lot of technical skill and know-how to get through the day. As a consequence of free markets, deregulation, and privatization, we as consumers have free choice of just about everything imaginable—and more. The basic consumer problem might still be to make enough money to be able to afford all the things we want, but that is mainly because there are so many things to want—and new things get added every day. We consumers have to learn new things daily from all the barrage. For example, I recently found out that cell phones now come with FM radio capability, in addition to cameras and Internet access. (I also learned not so long ago that telemarketers can get to me on my cell phone, perhaps hoping to sell me a financial package while hiking in unspoiled wilderness. But then again, why did I bring the phone with me and keep it on?)

Marketing saturation

That marketing infuses most aspects of our daily lives in the U.S. is, of course, not a very novel notion. Neither is it necessarily a force for evil; although its effect is probably not quite as beneficial as my colleagues and I first thought. Still, customer satisfaction questionnaires at hospitals, post offices, public schools, and government agencies probably do more good than harm. Even though they restrict our vaunted academic freedom, innovation, and risk-taking, the teacher evaluation questionnaires at our university have produced more student-friendly classrooms, more organized lectures, and less distant teachers. Movie audience research to determine the most desirable ending to teenage flicks, although seeming to compromise directors and scriptwriters, seems pretty harmless given the profit and semi-exploitative motivations of the producers to start with. The same might be true for the massive marketing efforts made by many mega-churches to attract audiences to their gospel.

Nevertheless, I guess even the most pragmatic and accommodating conscience might be forgiven for shuddering at the potential damaging effects from an omnipresent selling perspective. The temptation to shade an uncomfortable message in favor of positive news can compromise professional advice from doctors, lawyers, and yes, accountants. Hearing that National Public Radio (NPR), probably the single most important non-commercial broadcast news source in the U.S., bases its programming choices on market research aimed to identify target segments likely to contribute operating funds blurs the distinction with commercial stations and throws doubt on assumptions of objectivity.[3] Artistic integrity in art media with ambitions higher than entertaining teenagers is easily compromised when revenues and profits are the only guiding criteria. Robert Altman's *The Player*, a movie about moviemaking, cynically illustrates the corruption of artistic integrity by commercialism by ending the in-the-movie movie with Bruce Willis suddenly appearing to save the world. The Hollywood motto seems to be: "Insult the viewer's intelligence if you have to, but don't make him or her leave the theatre unhappy!"

Irresponsible marketing?

I tried to shrug off the queasy feeling about today's marketing. The Hummer was just one more example of the typical American way. But then, what was the American way? The Hummer ad seemed to be one more example of the kind of marketing effort that had produced the fast-food nation, the consumption craze of teenagers, and the most energy-wasting people on earth. It was another of the over-the-top marketing efforts that seemed to be necessary in a completely saturated marketplace, where wants and needs were continuously recreated rather than met. I already

---

3. *The Washington Post*, April 12, 2002, p. C01. On the other hand, the
    financial pressure on NPR is considerable. Accusing NPR of "profound
    anti-Israeli bias," the Committee for Accuracy in Middle East Reporting
    in America (CAMERA) demanded that NPR's foreign editor be removed
    because of his "long record of partisanship in favor of Palestinian
    views." Even though NPR dismissed the accusations after review, at
    least one station, WBUR (FM) in Boston, lost underwriting funding and
    listener support.

knew that the U.S. spent vastly more in per-capita marketing expenditures than any other country. For example, in advertising expenditures alone, my own global marketing text showed that in 1999, the U.S. spent about $445 per capita, far ahead of second-place Japan with $262, the United Kingdom with $252, Germany with $230, and France with $157, the same as Canada.[4]

This big spending apparently has had some effect. I read that Americans have grown fat by eating more calories than their bodies can burn—one reason why bigger cars are attractive.[5] U.S. teenagers spent $155 billion in "discretionary income" in 2000 alone, mainly on clothes, cosmetics, and music, and companies have followed suit, increasing their spending on marketing to kids twenty-fold between 1989 and 1999.[6] As for energy usage, the American per-capita oil consumption in 1999 was 25 barrels, compared with 15.7 for Japan, and 12.4 for both France and Germany.[7]

So, what did this all mean to me? Was marketing alone to blame for these things? Weren't free markets and free choice the bases of the capitalist system? Even a judge had this to say: "If a person knows or should know that eating copious orders of super-sized McDonald's products is unhealthy and may result in weight gain ... it is not the place of the law to protect them from their own excesses ... nobody is forced to eat at McDonald's."[8]

---

4. Johny K. Johansson, *Global Marketing*, Third Ed. (Boston: McGraw-Hill/Irwin), 2003, p. 509.

5. One of many striking statistics in Eric Schlosser's best–selling book, *Fast Food Nation* (Houghton-Mifflin), 2001, is that while in 1991 only four states had obesity rates of 15% or higher, by 2001, at least 37 states did (p. 240).

6. From Alissa Quart's *Branded: The buying and selling of teenagers* (Perseus), 2003, pp. xiii, 51.

7. From *The Washington Times*, January 1, 2003, Wednesday, Final Edition, p. A12. Price differentials of course matter a lot too.

8. In January 2003, U.S. District Judge Robert Sweet dismissed a lawsuit against the fast-food giant.

Strike Two: Anti-Globalization

Like almost everyone I know, I was surprised and taken aback at the violent demonstrations against the World Trade Organization (WTO) meeting in Seattle in December 1999. Just a couple of months earlier, I had finished the second edition of my textbook on global marketing, and everything seemed to be going well—right on course—with the global economy. Even though Japan's economic malaise still lingered (ruining sales of my co-authored 1996 book on the Japanese way of marketing), other Asian economies, as well as Russia and Latin America, showed strength, having just shaken off some bad financial crises. The Europeans were still moving forward, having introduced the Euro common currency for credit transactions earlier in the year, and getting ready for bills and coins to come on January 1, 2002. The magic of the semi-conductor economy, the Internet, and the dot-coms showed little or no evidence of weakness, and America had lived up to its promise of riches for everyone—especially for those invested in the stock market. The only real worry was the predicted large-scale computer failures with the arrival of the new millennium. But even so, everything seemed to be under control (one of those rare cases where a government-organized effort seemed to have really worked without a glitch).

Of course, the newspapers and other media reports from Seattle focused on the broken windows, the looted stores, and the police ineptitude. Predictably, observers denounced the attacks as being incited by fringe elements, outsiders, and troublemakers, including many foreigners. In my eyes, this was to be expected and did not diminish the impact of the demonstrations. I had been a student at Berkeley in the 1960s and had seen with my own eyes how news reports necessarily play up the sensational elements of an event, however well-organized and peaceful, misleading outsiders. In 1964, in Berkeley, the early allegations were that communists and foreign students inspired the anti-Vietnam demonstrations. The Seattle demonstrators were not denounced as communists, but they were grouped together as "foreigners and radicals."

One reason why I found the demonstrations significant was that in my global marketing text, I had warned managers against the blind implementation of what many called "the global imperative." For most of my colleagues, globalization was an imperative: "Go global or die!" As it is, today's typical management and marketing books still take for granted that the appropriate strategy for most products and services involves international expansion. Growth markets are found abroad. Naturally, an academic textbook has to follow the mainstream line of thought.

But, in my own text, I had deviated slightly from this single-minded drive to expand abroad. One reason was that I had doubts about the benefits brought to the various countries entered. As global marketers, my MBA students would be expected to "bring good things to life," as touted in GE's oft-repeated advertising slogan. But, in many cases, it was not clear that the products and services they would be selling were needed in the local markets. As Bill Gates found when he went to South Africa after the end of apartheid, personal computers and Microsoft software were not the first, or even the second, priority for the people there.

There was also the question of different cultures. Not all people could be expected to be happy and pleased if fast-food restaurants crowded out local eateries, making traditional specialties harder to find. Of course, these and similar concerns ought to be recognized before trying to introduce new products, but it was clear that the global imperative made such finer points irrelevant. After all, with globalization, all countries would sooner or later need PCs, and people's eating habits would gradually change. It seemed more important to capture first-mover advantages and to be an inside player as each market took off— as it supposedly would. As any cultural anthropologist will tell you, local traditions and views are not necessarily accommodating to foreigners. I thought of Procter & Gamble's difficulty in developing the disposable diaper market in Japan with bulky American-style Pampers, boasting convenience for tired mothers taking care of baby "problems." A Japanese mother stays home; her baby is not a "problem." And the baby should look neat, not like a big hulk—factors recognized by local followers Kao and Uni-Charm, which quickly took major market shares.

The global marketer

I have always thought of global marketers as the flag-bearers of free trade and globalization. To use a metaphor, they are vassals in the service of capitalism, the first troops to attack when formerly closed markets open. If the chief executive officers (CEOs) of American multinationals were prodding the government and WTO to keep markets abroad open and free, it was the American marketers who launched the assaults, hawking their global brands. Marketing was a people business, people dealing with other people—lots of them—often across cultures. When you saw and felt globalization, it was because marketers had put their brands and promotions in places you would never have expected them, such as on big billboards for Sony in Pamplona's bullfight arena in Spain. In any case, the Multilateral Agreement on Investment (MAI), the OECD and WTO attempt to free global investment flows, had already failed a couple of years earlier. The globalization march was clearly spearheaded by the global marketers of products and services, especially the Americans, the Europeans, and the Japanese.

I knew that most advanced marketing tools and techniques had been developed in the U.S. It was only natural that global marketers from the U.S. would be the most aggressive users of marketing when going abroad. In some ways, marketing has always existed. To use a slightly tired but illustrative example, even practitioners of the oldest profession in the world, prostitutes, discovered ways to display their wares. Excavations have uncovered Pompeiian tablets promulgating the advantages of certain medicines. Even warranties were extended—and enforced. When a colleague of mine returned from newly opened China, he reported that in the case of the large cobblestones laid in the Forbidden City, each had the stone mason's signature engraved on it. He was told that if a stone split, so would the mason's head, making "the punishment fit the crime." Today's marketers might use more sophisticated tools, but the essentials are the same. And in the U.S. in particular, with its diversity, multiculturalism, and free-speech protection, the marketing effort has reached new heights every year during my 30-plus years here, and it has become increasingly difficult for any one voice to make itself heard in the overall din.

Having studied foreign markets in the West and the East, I knew that the noisy hard-sell of the American way of marketing might be a potential problem abroad. The Americans were not only armed with the latest weapons in advertising and sales promotion—using the new media, cross-marketing films and merchandise, creating promotional events, and so on—they also had the conviction that globalization more or less meant that the American way was winning. After all, with privatization, deregulation, and the fall of the Berlin Wall, communist and social-democratic alternatives to American capitalism had been conquered. What, with the American tendency to celebrate victories and any "Number 1" status in your face, at least some Americans were likely to show signs of hubris and braggadocio in foreign markets. Some foreign people certainly would be resentful; they would try to put up obstacles to the incursion and display "Schadenfreude" when and if the Americans faltered. I was not surprised to hear that in 1992, McDonald's was forced by a court to change its styrofoam packaging to more environmentally healthy packaging in Germany, that Indian farmers had ransacked a Kentucky Fried Chicken (KFC) restaurant in 1994, claiming that the chicken was contaminated, and that Nike had created a furor when it became the sole sponsor of the Brazilian soccer team in 1998.[9] But these seemed to be isolated incidents, small bumps in the globalization road. On the whole, throughout the 1990s, the global imperative was pretty much just that, an imperative.

Anti-globalization and branding

Globalization continued to encounter setbacks throughout 2000 and later. In 2000, the annual World Bank and International Monetary Fund (IMF) meeting in Washington, D.C. was cancelled. At the 2001 Genoa meeting of the eight leading Western economies,

---

9.   Johansson, pp. 7, 541

there were disruptions and one demonstrator was shot and killed.[10] The WTO meeting in Doha, Qatar in the spring of 2002 bowed to pressure from anti-globalization forces and eased restrictions on the generic production of critical drugs for third-world countries.

It is clear that the demonstrations have increased significantly in the past couple of years and the protests are having an effect. What's happened? Has the situation gotten much worse? Do protesters have more time? My sense is that the "honeymoon" for globalization in the wake of the fall of the Berlin Wall in 1989 is finished. People are tired of waiting for the fruits to be shared. What are global marketers doing wrong? The answer seems to lie in their emphasis on global branding.

Perhaps the most significant marketing development throughout the 1990s was the recognition that for many multinational companies, their major asset was simply their global brand name. As mergers and acquisitions were used to build presence in new markets, company executives and their lawyers needed to assess the financial worth of a potential takeover target. Since this worth was basically the discounted value of future income streams, there was a need to project future sales. Forecasting future sales involved projecting market share based on competitive advantage. A strong brand rather than physical assets and other balance sheet items consistently figured as an important advantage. Gradually, managers and analysts realized that for many global companies, their one key asset was their brand. A company like Coca-Cola found early on that its financial worth was almost entirely summed up by the worth of its brand, in 2002 about $70 billion.[11]

Building and leveraging brand value became a preoccupation not only for brand managers at middle management levels, but it reached all the way to the top of the organization. And, since

---

10. *The New York Times*, July 21, 2001, *www.nytimes.com/2001/07/21/ international/21ital.html*

11. From *Interbrand*'s annual ranking of the world's most valuable brands, *http://interbrand.com/surveys.asp*

building a brand was expensive, it was more efficient to leverage an existing brand by extending the brand to related products, and by expanding into new markets. Extending a brand to new products carries its own risks. Coca-Cola had been singularly unsuccessful with its efforts to go outside the soft-drink category, and instead expanded further into foreign markets. Global brands came to symbolize the march of globalization.

This brand expansion strategy met with resistance in many places. Anti-globalization had an anti-branding component to it. Global brands, because of their prominence, became convenient targets in anti-globalization attacks. In addition to the McDonald's outlets attacked in France and the KFC restaurants ransacked in India, there were boycotts of Nike and Disney, for their allegedly exploitative labor practices. I knew that less well-known brands employed similar practices. Levi's and Starbucks were being disparaged over the global communication networks, apparently for destroying local businesses. And the contamination problems of giant Coca-Cola in Belgium made headlines everywhere. Yes, brand equity had been built for these global giants, and it had come back to haunt them.

Maybe I was biased, but it was striking how these brands were all American. I had done a fair amount of research and writing on Japanese and European businesses and their brand-building efforts. I could see very little antagonism roused against them—nobody hit Sony or Honda; nobody complained about Nokia or Volvo; and even Mercedes and BMW, given the once-over at home in Germany for environmental insensitivity, seemed globally exempt. I knew that some of these foreign companies did bend over backward to be environmentally sound—Honda and its electric car project, for example—and might pay more attention to their workers—Volvo's plant in Kalmar, Sweden used a team concept to avoid numbingly repetitive tasks. Still, it was a real stretch for me to believe that only American companies did bad things.

Anti-Americanism was probably part of the anti-globalization package even before the Bush administration took office. The frequent allegations reported in the news media that the WTO, the

World Bank, and IMF were all puppets dominated by the U.S. only confirmed this. It also helped explain why my American colleagues—and I—seemed less cognizant of the anti-globalization issues and movement. We had chalked it up to the anti-Americanism inspired by the now sole superpower. We were the natural bully and our brands could be attacked, while the others were underdogs, and thus attacking those brands would be counterproductive. I could see this in another way: There were few or no attacks against other American brands such as Burger King, New Balance, Wrangler, and Pepsi. You attack the biggest, not the lesser brands, unless you want to risk a sympathy backlash.

No generation gap?

Another striking point was that there seemed to be no gender difference, and no generation gap, in the anti-globalization movement. I thought there would not be many highly educated people involved. Educated people tend to gain the most from globalization's demand for knowledge workers, and global business puts a premium on language and communication skills. Still, it was clear that the anti-globalization forces did not lack in intellectual power—quite the contrary. In addition to college students and union members, their ranks included a range of well-educated people from scientists and academicians to managers and professionals. These were not simply people who were thrown out of a job, but people who seemed genuinely alarmed about the environment and other globalization negatives.

The lack of a generation gap was most puzzling. On the surface, I would have expected the anti-globalization appeal to be stronger among the older generations. It was simply that laid-off workers tend to be older, that folding businesses are likely to be old and are known to protect locals, and that older people are generally less open to innovation and change. Also, from a marketing perspective, one would expect anti-commercialization sentiments to be stronger among older people. Protection of the local culture would seem an older person's concern, the intense promotion of global brands for younger people would be noise to older people, and younger people would be happy about the excitement brand marketers create.

Judging from photos and newspaper reports, why were so many of the anti-globalization demonstrators so young? Was it simply a matter of energy and time—they had nothing better to do and needed to get rid of pent-up energy? Anyway, the young have always been against their parents and the "establishment." This seemed the favored explanation among many conservative observers. The fact was that many young workers, especially those less skilled, were also among the laid-off from firms under pressure from global competitors. Because of this, they did have time and energy, if not money. And they were likely to be single, not constrained by family obligations as married couples might be.

This could not be the whole story, however. For the fact was that many of these young people seemed very sincere, sometimes religious, and were still in high school or college. In many ways, they were prime beneficiaries of globalization benefits, used to ethnic and racial diversity and able to move easily in different cultures. They were the kind of people able to use modern communication tools—mobile phones, e-mail, and the Internet—to help organize demonstrations and coordinate activities. They also traveled light, and were thus able to cheaply travel to the different places around the world where the demonstrations occurred, including the huge January 2002 gathering in Porto Alegre, Brazil—not the easiest location to reach. And they were communicating using all available media, including music, the traditional avenue for protest.

My older daughter played for me a track on a CD with the music of a band from one of the many private high schools in the Washington area. The lyrics of the track, entitled "The STOP Song," advocated a rejection of the shopping and consumption lifestyle stimulated by the typical brand marketing messages. "Stop eating at McDonald's, stop drinking Coca-Cola," and so on. Judging from my 18-year-old daughter and her peers, the song reflected how at least some in the younger generation viewed globalization. There was apparently a nagging sense that the affluence of their lives came at the expense of suffering elsewhere, and despite the assurances that globalization was a win for all, the failings in third-world countries were too obvious to ignore. The "in-your-face" style of branded products and messages grated on teenagers at the front line of the brands' attacks, who were bombarded by advertisers and tired of the one-upmanship of their peers.

Strike Three: Anti-Americanism

Outside my office door at the university, I have a glass-covered posterboard where I can put up messages to my students. Because e-mail has pretty much eliminated the need to post class notices outside the office, I have taken to using the posterboard as more of a newsstand, putting up magazine headlines and articles relevant to my courses. Since I mainly teach global business and marketing, most of the postings refer to international developments, including anti-globalization news. Since 9/11, however, most of the clippings have dealt with the political fallout from the terrorist attacks. And, to put it bluntly, most of them are now even more anti-global than the anti-globalization postings they replaced.

In-your-face politics

One posting described the 2001 U.S. rejection of the Kyoto Protocol on global warming, which had been signed on America's behalf by then-Vice President Gore. Because of strong environmental sentiments, this agreement had been particularly important to Germany and France, two key partners in Europe. President Bush was well aware of this importance, but refused to address their concerns, simply stating that the protocol was flawed and the U.S. would in time (no promised deadline, though) propose its own version of an agreement. Another newspaper clipping dealt with Bush's revocation of then-President Clinton's signing of the charter for the International Criminal Court in The Hague, justified by the fear that American soldiers and their superiors might be prosecuted by politically motivated foreigners. In logical consequence, I also posted news of the detention of suspected Al Qaeda terrorists in the Guantanamo Bay military base without legal recourse.

The postings suggested that the American administration was willing to thumb its collective nose at international allies in other ways as well. Any free trade commitment of the government vanished as new tariffs as high as 30% were imposed on steel imports from Europe, New Zealand, and other countries. Not unexpectedly, the WTO ruled the tariffs illegal under its trade rules. The American agriculture industry received steep new subsidies, thoroughly compromising the efforts to help third-world countries reap some gains from globalization (although here, the Europeans were surely also to blame). A less depressing, but still relevant, clipping was a tongue-in-cheek column from *Time* magazine by Joel Stein about the 2002 World Cup in Japan/Korea, in which America's lack of interest in the "rest-of-the-World Cup" tournament was blamed on weak marketing and zero brand tie-ins.[12]

These decisions set the stage for the confrontations we all saw leading up to the Iraq war. I did not post any clippings from that period. They seemed redundant since all news sources focused on the United Nations (UN), France, Germany, Tony Blair, and the anti-war demonstrations anyway. The UN was derided and ultimately bypassed by the Americans. Leading representatives of the U.S. government made a point of scorning disagreeing allies, exacerbating diplomatic friction, and creating more international tension.

The list of anti-international actions is daunting for someone like myself who makes a living teaching young—and not-so-young—people to adopt an international and tolerant outlook. This is not the kind of behavior that I have taught my students. I am not against politics again taking on a more prominent role than economics and free trade in international affairs. And I am not necessarily against conservatives on political grounds. But these actions, increasingly legitimized on the basis of the 9/11 attacks, were carried out with a unilateral and arrogant zeal—the kind of "in-your-face" attitude that reminded me of an athlete's "trash talk." Most of these actions had reasonable and reasoned justifi-

---

12. *Time*, June 17, 2002, p. 88.

cations that could and should have been articulated. The evidence was that some of the early decisions—the rejection of the Kyoto Protocol and the International Criminal Court, for example—might well have been chosen by Clinton as well, but that the diplomacy would have been much less "in your face." It was clearly unnecessary to engage in the kind of belligerent attitude that was evidenced. From where did this attitude emerge?

Anti-American fallout

My research assistant checked out the data on anti-American fallout. As one could have predicted, the indicators of how others viewed the U.S. and its policies showed a dramatic drop. The Pew Research Center, in its large-scale survey of global attitudes, showed that in numerous countries, the U.S. image dropped precipitously between summer 2002 and March 2003 (Table 1.1).[13] The countries included in both years show the following percentages of favorable respondents:

TABLE 1.1   Percent of Respondents Favorable Toward the U.S.

Country	2002	2003
Britain	75%	48%
France	63%	31%
Germany	61%	25%
Italy	70%	34%
Spain	50%	14%
Poland	79%	50%
Russia	61%	28%
Turkey	30%	12%

The average decline is from 61% to 30%, a precipitous drop, especially considering that Britain, Spain, and Poland officially supported the war. Equally striking is the reflection in American

---

13. *Views of a Changing World* (Washington: The Pew Research Center for the People & the Press) June 2003, pp.T-132,133.

attitudes toward traditional allies. Between February 2002 and summer 2003, the Pew data (Table 1.2) show the following changes in the Americans' evaluation of the three countries for which comparable data are available:[14]

TABLE 1.2 Percent of Americans Favorable Toward Foreign Countries

Country	2002	2003
Britain	90%	82%
France	79%	29%
Germany	83%	44%

The average drop among the Americans is from 84% to 52%. These are sobering figures to say the least. Sure, public opinion is not what wins wars, and what people think can change quickly. But, in another sense, military victories can be hollowed by resentment, and some of these sentiments are not necessarily just temporary. Most likely, the overseas reactions involved some emotions and beliefs that were rekindled by American belligerence. One can think of events such as the exoneration of the American fighter pilot in the Italian alps, who caused the death of some 20 skiers in 1998,[15] the reluctant remorse of the submarine commander who accidentally rammed a Japanese fishing vessel

---

14. Ibid, p. T-132.
15. The pilot was acquitted of manslaughter, but sentenced to six months in military prison for destroying a videotape shot during the flight. The navigator was dismissed from the Marines after pleading guilty to a similar charge regarding the videotape's disappearance. Charges were dropped against the two backseat crewmen. Italians were incensed at the judicial outcome. Then-Premier Romano Prodi said it was an "earth-shaving flight," a "terrible act," and an Italian parliamentary investigative commission concluded the American airmen had acted as criminals. Since then, the families of each victim, all European, have received about $1.5 million in compensation, 70% from the U.S. government and 30% from the Italian government, said Werner Pichler, a spokesman for a group formed by the families. Doug Simpson, "Canadian Bombing Incident Parallels Marines' Deadly Italian Ski-Lift Flight," *The Associated Press State & Local Wire*, January 23, 2003.

in 2001, killing nine on-board,[16] and the initially covered-up rape of a 12-year-old schoolgirl outside an American base on Okinawa in 1995. These and other events might in some ways be unavoidable given American military presence abroad; but nevertheless, they give glimpses of a national character that is not always as pure as its public pronouncements suggest. As a Canadian said after the Northeast blackout in August 2003, "Have you ever seen the United States take the blame for anything?"[17] Other countries might not be much better, but these transgressions are made worse by the way they are typically handled in America. Initial denial and aggressive defiance—"talk to my lawyer"—make belated shows of sincerity and remorse seem hypocritical and shameless. Benjamin Franklin's concept and promotion of America's unique moral standing in the world can easily be corrupted by sanctimonious and pompous rhetoric.

The "In-Your-Face" Spin

By now, I really felt a need to try to put the anti-marketing, anti-globalization, and anti-American movements in perspective. These were challenges to what I had believed for a long time. I had left my native Sweden for graduate school in America, sponsored by the Ford Motor Company. I stayed on not because the country seemed to offer more freedom and opportunity—to me, Sweden in the 1960s was ahead of the U.S. on both counts, believe it or not. No, I stayed on because this country was more fun. Compared to Sweden, it was—and is still—young, doing things was more important—and still is—than reflecting on them, and energy still beat brains, even among professionals. Actions spoke louder than words—and still do, and a lot of energy was—

---

16. The families of 33 people who were aboard the Japanese fishing trawler agreed in 2002 to a reported $13 million compensation package from the U.S. Navy. Chris Weelock, "U.S. Navy Completes Final Settlement in Ehime Maru Incident," *CNN.com*, February 1, 2003.

17. Toronto mayor Mel Lastman, after the blackout also reached Canada, as reported by *Time*, August 25, 2003, p.17.

and still is—wasted, all in the name of excitement, challenge, and fun, fun, fun. All this was very attractive.

Of course, being a professor also seemed a pretty good job judging from the activists on the Berkeley faculty in the 1960s. Plus, with all the excitement, marketing was something that America was good at. When Japan showed in the 1980s that it could do even better, I spent a lot of time "doing Japan," watching it turn to global marketing as globalization progressed through the 1990s. If there is a sense of opportunism here that goes badly with what professors should be about, I confess to that. Teaching in a business school involves staying in touch with economic (and sometimes political) developments, and colors what one ends up researching.

Now reality had checked all of that. Here I was in America, writing about global marketing and the value of a global power brand, while at the same time activists (and my daughters' schoolmates) trashed the brands. I was teaching budding marketing students how to get into foreign markets and establish "beachheads," drawing on their competitive advantages over domestic producers to penetrate local markets. I taught case studies on how Levi's became the leading jeans-maker in Japan by positioning itself as the "original" American cowboy gear, how McDonald's brought its arches to Russia after the fall of the Berlin Wall, and how Nike moved aggressively into sponsoring popular sports overseas, like soccer, which Americans seemed to have little interest in. Were these just benevolent strategic efforts, which although they surely helped the companies' bottom lines, also provided great benefits for the customers in the different countries? Or, were they just efforts from an increasingly unilateral American attitude to dominate foreign markets?

It all seemed so much "in your face." In a way, I liked the expression, since it signified an irreverent attitude, a confrontation against some opponent, a challenge to authority. It represented a stance against someone, overcoming a real or imagined foe. The "We're number 1" sign used by athletes is one early version. It's associated with the face-to-face confrontation one sometimes sees between athletes trash-talking each other's game.

In earlier and more sentimental days, in-your-face behavior was associated with the underdog confronting a supposedly stronger foe. In this sense, Mickey Rooney, the perky film comedian, who could be accused of always playing in-your-face roles, was also embraced by audiences partly because of his short stature. By contrast, in-your-face attitudes by individuals who had the advantage were always punished. One can think of the countless German officers in World War II films whose dire fate was preordained as they "in your faced" some allied prisoner of war. Today, of course, such niceties are gone. Airs of superiority by advantaged players not only go unpunished, any negative connotations of arrogance and bullying attached to such behavior have given way to approval and supportive smirks. Good sportsmanship has gone down in direct proportion to athletes' paychecks going up.

Today there is more to the in-your-face attitude. It reflects an unwillingness to accept an opponent as an equal, and a rejection of any claims on his or her behalf. That is, "I am right and you are wrong." There is no need for a dialogue; there is actually no need for me to listen to you. If one recognizes some of the typical teenager's slant to this, as most parents would, it is clear that the in-your-face attitude reflects an immature and insecure personality. Complexities and uncertainties are ignored and denied. Things are black and white; there are no gray areas. It is, of course, not a very long step to the fundamentalism of various religious cults.

It was this aspect of in-your-face airs that made me cringe when seeing the Hummer ad. It played directly to the kind of infantile feelings that presumably many people have overcome. "Get this car and get in other people's faces" was the message conveyed. The copy was not simply in my face; it exhorted me to be in other people's faces—and to enjoy it. The advertising was an insult to me because of the product appeal used—plus it exhorted me to be insulting to other people. Was this what I had been teaching all these years?

2 THE ANTI-MARKETING CASE

Less is more.

The contents of a weekly magazine are perhaps not the most accurate indicator of what a nation is concerned about. But in its issue for the week of April 28, 2003, just as the war in Iraq was coming to an end, Time *magazine featured a three-page article on telemarketing entitled "Stop Calling Us" (the Iraq coverage netted 12 pages, plus photos).*[1] *The article stated that telemarketing calls had been growing from 18 million in 1991 to a projected 104 million in 2003. No wonder I felt attacked. And I was apparently not alone in trying to stem the tide—the writers detailed a number of new devices designed to thwart the offenders. In addition to the TeleZapper I received as a gift, there is the Phone Butler, the Privacy Manager, and the Screen Machine; and then there is Caller ID and stringent new privacy laws on some states' books. A friend of mine in Sweden sent me the information sheet for that country's solution: a cost-free registration service maintained by a business for which a household signs up and with which telemarketers have to check before calling—leave it to the Swedes to be reasonable! Now of course, the U.S. has instituted its own DoNotCall.com registry—there's always hope. The article finished on a pessimistic note, how-*

---

1.   Perry Bacon, Jr,. and Eric Roston, "Stop Calling Us: How to TKO Telemarketers," *Time*, April 28, 2003.

ever. For every new device so far, the telemarketers' technology wizards have devised ways around the obstacle. And somebody once said that technology is neutral!

In the following week's issue, May 5, Time's *coverage of the Iraq war was down to three pages, plus pictures, but the marketing expose had been ramped up to a four-page feature on captive marketing entitled "There's No Escape."[2] I was embarrassed, not because of the content—which was bad enough (as you will see below)—but because I had not heard the term "captive marketing" before. I teach the stuff; I should know it. As it turned out, my assistant was ahead of me. He knew about captive marketing first-hand.*

My assistant is a newly minted MBA who is mainly busy looking for a better-paying job in a down economy. He likes to soothe his employment blues at Capitol City Brewing Company, a small microbrewery bar and restaurant in his Alexandria neighborhood. He told me that on his rather frequent visits to the urinal stall, he comes face-to-face with a TV screen advertising local offerings. As he goes about his business, these kinds of messages scroll by on the screen:

"Have you thought of bringing our micro-beer home? We've got a two-liter keg for you. Have you left room for our homemade desserts? If not, you may want to make some room. They're delicious."

"Gross," we both agreed. "Literally in your face." But, captive marketing is just one of the new marketing "tools" and at the beginning of its lifecycle. You'll find these invasive video screens in an increasing number of places. Apart from restrooms, now elevators, hospital beds, taxis, buses, gas station self-service pumps, shopping malls, department stores, stadiums, and movie theaters, of course, all provide the kind of semi-captive audience with nothing better to do than watch a video clip— and the advertisers are pounding. You might have thought advertising was everywhere already, but it seems we have not seen anything yet.

---

2.   Michele Orecklin, "There's No Escape," *Time,* May 5, 2003.

The Anti-Marketing Movement

Anti-marketing sentiments in the U.S. are not really very new. For a long time, the hucksterism associated with selling and advertising has made charges of deceit and unscrupulousness come natural to many critics of marketing. For example, *subliminal advertising*, where selling messages are surreptitiously inserted into a movie frame or where alluring images are embedded into advertisements, has long been viewed as unethical. *Target marketing*, the development of products and messages specifically tailored for a segment of the market, has also come under attack when used to sell alcohol to minorities, cigarettes to young people, and candy to children on Saturday morning cartoons. Camel cigarette's targeting of underage, potential smokers with the Joe Camel icon, now ceased under a court order, is perhaps one of the more egregious examples of abusive marketing.

Organized efforts to stimulate increased regulation of marketing practices have also emerged. They include governmental efforts, such as the consumerism movement initiated by then-President Kennedy, and the Federal Trade Commission's effort to control cigarette advertising, as well as efforts by non-governmental institutions such as Ralph Nader's Green Party and various centers for responsible citizenship. These efforts not only involve breaches of acceptable standards of safety and health in the products advertised, but also regulate specific marketing practices. One example is the "bait-and-switch" tactic, where a featured special is "out of stock" and a more expensive model is suggested. Many initiatives constrain advertising practices such as placing limits on children's TV advertising, abolishing cigarette billboards in sports arenas, restricting liquor advertising, demanding proof-of-advertising claims, and prosecuting misleading advertising.

Today's anti-marketing attacks take on a much broader target—the materialism and commercialism permeating all of society. As free markets make inroads into an increasing number of institutions previously insulated—hospitals, universities, sports teams, city governments, gas companies, electric utilities, post offices—marketing seems to be everywhere. Doctors, police officers, and professors become *de facto* salespeople—of themselves, of their organization, of their profession. This is not good for professional integrity or trust.

Not surprisingly, as a marketing perspective spreads, it inspires increasingly vociferous anti-marketing protests. Even though commercialism may not yet be a mainstream concern, the *Time* coverage suggested it may soon be. Anti-marketing sentiments can be found not just among the "usual suspects" of the liberal left, but among the extreme right wing (who worry about the erosion of fundamental values), as well as among middle-ground professionals (who are concerned about the "every person has a price" implications).

The new anti-marketing

If you want a starting date for today's increasingly broad-based anti-marketing sentiment, you might choose September 15, 1997. That was the day when the Public Broadcasting Station (PBS) first aired the TV program *Affluenza*, a documentary about the materialistic and commercialized lifestyle of the typical American family. The program, featuring interviews with individuals, families, and psychologists, and drawing on published data on quality-of-life indicators, painted a bleak picture of the American way of life. The program detailed the American family's preoccupation with shopping, buying, using and discarding products, and how life had become dominated by the desire for ever more possessions. It decried the excessive consumption of unhealthy foods, the wasteful use of energy, the advertising blitzes targeting younger family members, all leading to the feelings of spiritual emptiness and lack of meaning expressed by the supposedly happy consumers. The blight of the ensuing wasteland was succinctly expressed by a program participant: "Dissatisfaction guaranteed."

The program drew a strong response from viewers, and apparently touched a deep nerve of concern. In response, a follow-up book was produced, which quickly became a bestseller.[3] The pro-

---

3.   John de Graaf, David Wann, and Thomas H. Naylor, *Affluenza: The All-consuming Epidemic* (San Francisco: Berrett-Koehler), 2001.

gram and the ensuing book actually did not attack marketing or advertising practices per se. The target was the way the economy had become a self-serving machine. We lived to consume; we did not consume to live. But this theme was of course a main preoccupation and result of marketing activities, and subsequent books and articles came to focus more directly on those activities.

Advertising messages are one of the building blocks that constitutes the massive commercializing trend in our society. But the start is really with the availability of products everywhere. These in-your-face strategies include intensive distribution with rollouts of products into all major distribution points (Levi's, Nike), and the new development of dense networks of distribution outlets (Starbucks, McDonald's). Products are now available in more locations and stores are open longer hours than ever. Not only are there more shopping malls with more stores and amenities than ever, the various brands are available in a wider variety of stores, from their own boutiques, to department stores, to discount stores and factory outlets, to warehouse outlets—not to mention gray goods, pirated copies, and counterfeits. Sure, some brands follow more limited distribution strategies to enhance their exclusivity, and even the same brand sometimes produces slightly different versions for its own boutiques, but essentially, in the U.S., you can buy almost anything at any time of the day if you really want to. Online shopping means that you can buy a used car or a new camera, survey the new fashions, do your banking, and reserve an airplane ticket any time of the day (and night). To use a marketing phrase: "You've come a long way, baby!"

As for advertising, it isn't just that promotional messages can reach you through all the media, old—TV, radio, newspapers, magazines, outdoors—and new—the telephone, the Internet, e-mail, the cell phone. Using the multiple available media, from one-to-one marketing to the Internet to mass media advertising, promotional campaigns include saturation advertising and point-of-purchase sales promotions, with tie-ins to events and sponsorships. Publicity is generated by the use of press conferences and new product demonstrations. The aim is literally to make it impossible to escape the hype—even for those of us who are not in the market or even in the target market. It's literally in-your-face marketing.

In 1999, the founder of *Adbusters*, Kalle Lasn, published his *Culture Jam* book, vowing to reverse America's suicidal consumer binge.[4] The book was a call to arms of sorts, describing "Buy Nothing Days" and inciting "culture jammers" to not only stop consuming, but to actively sabotage marketing efforts (including spray-painting over billboard ads). The rebellious theme was taken up again in Naomi Klein's *No Logo* book in 2000.[5] Klein's main target was the dominant presence of powerful global brands in today's international marketplace, and how large corporations have used their financial and marketplace advantages to quash local competitors. Her catalog of proposals for global anti-brand actions—boycotting brands, disrupting shareholder meetings, and picketing at trade conferences—has, together with *Culture Jam*, become a kind of manifesto for the anti-marketing and anti-globalization forces.

In 2001, another book, Eric Schlosser's *Fast Food Nation*, took on a narrower target, the supplier relations and marketing practices of the companies behind the all-American hamburger meal.[6] Focusing on McDonald's, the book paints vivid portraits of the people behind the Big Mac and how their product has come to symbolize the American Way, including the resulting new highs in obesity levels. A similar indictment of the free market and its abuses was issued in the 2003 book *Branded* by Alissa Quart, which details in-depth the degree to which the American teenage market is over-run by companies eager to imprint their brand logos on the minds of their young customers.[7] Judging from the many personal interviews the author draws on, the teen rebellion

---

4. Kalle Lasn, *Culture Jam: How to Reverse America's Suicidal Consumer Binge—and Why We Must* (New York: Quill), 1999.
5. Naomi Klein, *No Logo* (London: Flamingo), 2000.
6. Eric Schlosser, *Fast Food Nation: The Dark Side of the All-American Meal* (Boston: Houghton-Mifflin), 2001.
7. Alissa Quart, *Branded: The Buying and Selling of Teenagers* (Cambridge, MA: Perseus), 2003.

against some of the more major brands—Nike, Gap, Starbucks—could soon extend further.

So what?

Meanwhile, in the profession, we marketers seemed to carry on with business pretty much as usual. True, for the brands attacked, the situations required damage control and some remedial actions—redesigning packages, adapting products, eliminating objectionable advertising—continued to be taken. In addition, public relations staff was augmented, ethical guidelines were promulgated, and presentable executives were made available to the media. But apart from these defensive actions by the particular brands attacked, nothing much had changed. The branding machine kept churning. Business books on how to build and manage brands were bestsellers. New books exhorted companies to unite behind global brands and listed strategies for how to eliminate local brand names without losing loyal customers. Newer branding mantras involved how to create brand-related "experiences," which linked an individual's sense of identity to a brand, and how to navigate profitably in the new "hyper-reality" of the "consumerspace." Few concerns were voiced in these books over negative consumer reactions, and when anti-branding actions were acknowledged, the books relied on standard suggestions for how to deal with disgruntled customers (like "Be sensitive!").

One reason for the discounting of the anti-marketing sentiment among professionals is the sense that the movement is from a vocal fringe minority of individuals. However, the overwhelming response to the DoNotCall.com registry has clearly invalidated this argument. One reason for the remaining complacency is the sense that the new era of one-to-one interactive marketing has changed the game in favor of the consumer. In 1993, a book by Don Peppers and Martha Rogers entitled *The One-to-One Future* hailed the arrival of one-to-one marketing, where customization to individual customers would be economically feasible on a mass scale.[8] Using direct mail, fax machines, touch-

---

8. Don Peppers and Martha Rodgers, *The One-to-One Future* (New York: Doubleday), 1993.

tone and cell phones, e-mail, interactive TV—and the Internet—messages, products, and services could be tailored to the needs and preferences of individual consumers, identified from address lists, credit records, purchase histories, and other available information. One-to-one marketing using these databases meant the end of the old mass-marketing techniques. Now only those consumers in the target demographic would be contacted, and only with offerings designed specifically for them. There would be no more wasted mailings or phone calls, and promotion dollars would be used more efficiently. Overall, it meant much less of the annoying advertising of completely irrelevant products for the average individual. This is known as *narrowcasting*, as opposed to broadcasting.

With the Internet also came interactive and consumer-initiated marketing. Consumers were now "empowered"—meaning they could initiate contact with a seller. Coupled with database marketing, the ground was cleared for a new and intimate connection between seller and buyer. *Relationship marketing* was applied over the computer and telephone lines, not just face-to-face. For instance, when you logged on to Amazon.com, you were recognized and greeted. Telemarketers, for all their invasive efforts, usually did offer something that would potentially fit into your own particular consumerspace. Direct marketing, even if not exactly one-on-one, was more efficient than mass mailings. And, despite the relative failure of the dot-com revolution and the flickering banner ads, e-commerce on the Web seemed to have some sustaining power. But, in parallel with this development, we were faced with the increasingly vociferous anti-marketing forces. How did this come about? Could these opposing forces be reconciled? One answer could be that they are, in fact, two sides of the same coin.

Not the same old...

One reason for professional complacency is that, in a sense, marketing has always been "in your face." Check out TV commercials from the 1950s and you'll find an enervating spokesperson, loud, annoying, and cheerful, promising long life and happiness if only you use this product and buy this brand. The model followed is, of course, even older than that. In *The Elixir of Love*, Gaetano Donizetti's still-popular opera premiered in 1832, the brand promise is that "Septuagenarians will make babies"—actually not a bad slogan for Viagra. The *Titanic* was boosted as "unsinkable." Over-promising, puffery, and shading the truth are not new promotional strategies.

What is new is mostly a matter of degree, an increase in the wattage used, and an extension of the media made available—broadly speaking, there is now an invasive effort to reach us anywhere and anytime. We can run, but we cannot hide. What is new is also the language used to talk to us, the willingness to shock, to use foul language, and to play as much on our secret fears and guilt as on our more wholesome and uplifting emotions of simply being able to acquire things that help to enjoy a better life. Pride, envy, and dominance over one's peers have always been part of the acquiring psyche, but these traits are now posited as major motivators behind many brand choices.

Adding to the increased noise is the vastly greater number of products and services now available, each of which demands attention from stressed-out individuals. Technology is, of course, one reason for the proliferation of products. You need only compare today's personal computer products, audio and video players, and telephones with what was available in the "more innocent" 1950s to get a sense of what technology has brought. Then there was the push toward deregulation and privatization initiated in the 1980s during the Reagan presidency. One result has been a dizzying array of choices facing a public used to a simpler life. The information needed to choose between healthcare providers, insurance carriers, telephone companies, mortgage lenders, gas versus electric power, buying or leasing a car, and so on is naturally provided by the private organizations profiting from the new market opportunities. No wonder sales pitches have become part and parcel of such information—and that one now needs to do some homework comparing alternatives. When more traditional choices—how to find a good dentist, in which hospital to have a baby, where to send your son or daughter to college, how to take care of your elderly parents—are factored in, it is not surprising to learn that Americans seem busier than ever. Life *was* simpler before.

The explanation for the increasing commercialization and incessant advertising anti-marketers complain about is not entirely a matter of bad intent on the part of marketers. They need to make themselves heard. It is easy to deplore the promotion of unhealthy foods and unsafe products, but the noise and the hoopla also involve less controversial products and services, including fundraising for good causes, symphony subscriptions, and the Girl Scouts. It all adds to the clutter—the clutter that in turn forces the advertisers to be even louder and more in your face. For the marketers too, it's a dog-eat-dog world. This is useful to remember if one wants to understand how we got into this mess. Before rejecting marketing outright, it is important to recognize that today's intense competition has helped make marketing practices what they are.

The Marketing Battlefield

The brand name and logo are today the major weapons in the marketing war between competitors. Since new technological advances diffuse rapidly, competitors can no longer differentiate simply on the basis of functional benefits. Any one special feature offers at best only a temporary market advantage. Taking several pages from their Japanese competitors' playbook, Western producers adopted the quality practices of "the best in the world," sped up the product-to-market cycle, reverse-engineered competitors' new products, and "benchmarked" the competition. If something worked well elsewhere, they used that as well—forget any old-fashioned hang-ups about "not invented here." Today there is a great deal of technological innovation and a high rate of new product introduction in categories as diverse as detergents, toothbrushes, shampoos, water, wines, sneakers, retailing, computers, even financial products. Is this good for the consumer? Yes, but when all competitors seem to offer the same thing, how can one choose? The marketer's answer is that we choose *where* to buy on price and *what* to buy on brand.

The sustainable competitive advantage in many industries has shifted from features and benefits to the brand name. "The brand equity is the firm's most valuable asset" is the new credo. Brand equity means not only brand image ("an upscale car," for example)—the old standby—but also brand meaning (What and who do you associate with the brand, outside of the product category?) and brand identity (What fundamental values does the brand stand for?). The brand is positioned as the consumer's "best friend." Building and managing the company brand is today a top management priority.

The result is predictable. As competitive advantages increasingly rest on the intangible associations evoked by a brand's images and allusions, consumers are over-run by hype and promotion. The battlefield trophy to capture is a dominant "share of mind" (or, as Pepsi has it, "share of stomach"), to create loyalty and affinity toward the brand, and to defend it staunchly by matching any promotional attack from competitors. Ideally, the brand name should be "tattooed" on the mind of the consumer—and, if at all possible, on the body, as widely admired marketer Harley-Davidson has managed with a number of its loyal customers. The strategy is really a variant of the old sales formula: "First make them notice you, then make sure they remember your name." And to get the attention of the prospects, it helps to be in their faces. Skydivers gulp soft drinks on their way down. A woman driving a Mercedes has something akin to an orgasm. Herbal Essences, an organic shampoo, is so great it delivers sexual satisfaction in the shower: "For a completely organic experience..." Stuntpeople die while shooting commercials. As one branding book has it: "Extreme times call for extreme measures."[9]

As physical product attributes and customer benefits become indistinguishable between competing offerings, and brand name associations are the only useful differentiations, the winner will be the brand that leaves the strongest impression. It is not surprising that this development dovetails with the increasing use of

---

9.   Kjell A. Nordstrom and Jonas Ridderstrale, *Funky Business* (Stockholm: Bookhouse Publishing), 1999, p. 83.

extreme sports and violent reality (although only virtual) footage in TV commercials for brands such as Mountain Dew. Benetton advertisements showing photos of AIDS patients and terrorist victims also fit this picture. A shock can leave an indelible impression—and inspire anti-marketing attitudes. It seems questionable whether such desperate marketing tactics ever help produce sales, but then, if they didn't, why would the companies keep using them?

Same new, same new

Then there is the sheer volume of it all. If anti-marketers feel inundated with identical commercial messages for new products or brands, the culprit is probably the new strategy of *integrated marketing communications*, or IMC for short. Centered on the brand, the basic idea behind this marketing mantra is simple: All promotional media through which a potential customer might come into contact with the brand should be used—and the messages should all be the same. In a narrow sense, IMC stands for the consistency of a brand's slogan and logo, wherever presented; but it has also come to mean the use of all available media for the projection of a brand. IMC represents a full-court press to advance a brand's assets. Today, the number of media through which a potential customer can be reached has multiplied.

Examples of the use of IMC are everywhere today. Disney was an early pioneer. A new Disney film such as *The Lion King*, for example, is advertised on the Disney TV channel, featured on the Disney Internet site, and cross-merchandised products and souvenirs are available in Disney stores. Carefully timed releases of the video and the production of a stage version for Broadway are launched with appropriate fanfare in news media. Publicity is generated through press releases and opening night extravaganzas. Global rollout is as rapid as possible to avoid piracy. Positive audience figures are released to emphasize the success of the new film.

Liquor brands, such as Dewar's whisky and Absolut vodka, have gotten into the act with launch parties, Internet chat rooms, in-bar promotions, and merchandise giveaways, in addition to regular media advertising. The Pokemon craze was launched according to the same principles, and of course, Microsoft's new Windows releases and Apple's new Macintosh models follow these patterns as well. But, the effort is not limited to only high-visibility brands. Today, IMC forms most brand promotions, from Colgate's new toothpaste to Sony's Playstation 2 to the Red Bull energy drink. It is perhaps not surprising that many brand managers, even in the most mundane businesses, seem to think they are in the entertainment business.

Other prime examples of IMC come from the automobile industry. The launch of a new car nowadays involves more than the traditional automobile exhibition and ensuing media promotion. The company Web site features the new car, with commercials and film clips. Videos are made available to dealers and prospective buyers. Direct mail and telemarketing may be used to target high-potential addresses from databank lists. Sports and other events may be sponsored or even created to attract more attention. Loaners or gifts to disc jockeys and TV personalities could provide extra exposure and endorsement. Celebrities—sports and movie stars—may be offered generous fees and contracts to use the car and to feature the car logo on outfits. For example, Arnold Schwarzenegger, with his appropriately outsized persona, is a spokesperson for Hummer. The campaign may even include product placement, with the car featured in a movie or TV series.[10] Organizations may be offered discounts for fleet purchases and the use of special-edition limos—and so on. In IMC, the only limitation is your imagination.

IMC has become a natural outgrowth and a reason for the consolidation of media conglomerates, the synergistic blending of hardware, transmission, and content. The success of IMC provides a rationale for integrated media businesses such as Viacom, as well as less successful mergers such as AOL-Time Warner (now with-

---

10. The launch of the BMW Z3 is a case in point, with the new roadster introduced as James Bond's new car in the *Golden Eye* film. See Susan Fournier and Robert J. Dolan, *Launching the BMW Z3 Roadster,* Harvard Business School case no. N9-597-002.

out the AOL logo) and Sony-Columbia pictures. Regardless of the financials, from a strict marketing viewpoint, the potential synergy is tempting (although the implementation is often complex). For the consumer and the latent anti-marketer, the hype is here, there, and everywhere.

Being "in the market"

As the *Affluenza* program documented thoroughly, wherever we go, we seem to be in one huge marketplace—"consumerspace," as a new book has it.[11] The impact of so many competing messages and products can range from excitement and fun to boredom and ennui or aversion and anger. It all depends on whether the commercials and products advertised are interesting or irrelevant to us, and whether the advertising is fun or annoying—and, most importantly, whether we are really in the market for that product just then.

You can fault promotional messages for being biased in favor of the brand advertised. Of course they are. You can also fault them for being "in your face," but again, this is not surprising given the competitive situation and saturated marketplace. The product advertised better be good and better deliver on the promises made, which is why we need regulations against misleading advertising. But, what determines our reaction is whether we are in the market when the message arrives.

When I go into a restaurant, I don't mind getting recommendations about the menu—I am "in the market." When I go to a car dealership, information about autos is useful. I am there for a test drive. When I log on to Amazon.com, I don't mind getting suggestions about books—that's what I am there for. But, I don't want to hear about restaurant food after I have eaten; I don't need information about a new car after I just bought one; and I don't need Amazon.com to tell me about credit cards. I am not in that market any-

11. Michael R. Solomon, *Conquering Consumerspace: Marketing Strategies for a Branded World* (New York: Amacom), 2003. A similar concept is "consumerscape" as coined by Russ Belk and his collaborators. See, e.g., Guliz Ger and Russell W. Belk, "I'd Like to Buy the World a Coke: Consumerscapes of the Less Affluent World," *Journal of Consumer Policy*, Vol.19, pp. 271–304.

more. As Macbeth, upon the news of his Lady's death, says: "There would have been a time for such a word. Tomorrow...."

Yes, there are times when new information coming surreptitiously is interesting and useful. But by and large, I want information when I decide I want it—just like one-to-one marketing and the Web sites promised, but failed to deliver. I want to be in control of when to receive information about new products, not get a sudden interruption from a telemarketing call at dinnertime or a pop-up ad on the Internet blocking my view of the screen. We are overwhelmed by commercialization because commercial messages can be beamed to us all the time, everywhere. With the intense competition between brands, marketers are forced to use their IMC arsenal fully, not simply when we empowered consumers want to hear their message.

Marketing spam

Even if we are not anti-marketing, the marketplace noise from the car radio, the TV, the telephone, and the computer makes us annoyed, surly, and short-tempered. It is like e-mail spam, only through all media. As with spam, we develop defense strategies. We all know what they might be. We play mood music on the car CD player, block incoming calls, don't answer the doorbell, throw away all direct mail; we get an ad-zapper for the TV, unsubscribe to magazines, stop buying annoying brands, and stop patronizing stores that don't feature generics. We do, in fact, opt out of certain segments of the marketplace. The problem is that in doing so, we might also end up opting out of things that we would like to support. The bad crowds out the good by usurping the channels through which we get information.

Blocking incoming calls might eliminate fundraising possibilities for charities we believe in. Not answering the doorbell means not being neighborly. Throwing away direct mail without opening it means our favorite radio station does not get supported. Zapping TV commercials slows new product information. Canceling subscriptions to magazines with advertisements from offending clients eliminates a news source. Stopping the purchase of brands with large advertising budgets means we might miss the best brand in the market.

This crowding-out problem results from what might be called a "majority fallacy." We as consumers reap the benefit from the intense competition between several competitors in an industry. But, when the intensity occurs across all the various products and services in today's marketplace, the din can cause overload. In addition, as the times *when* you can be reached as well as *how* you can be reached multiply, the result is the kind of situation we have today. When you are in the market, it all makes sense. When you are not in the market, it is all noise, quite literally.

In the end, I am not surprised to hear that so many Americans spend most of their free time shopping. Even with the Internet, telemarketing, catalog sales, supermarkets, and city boutiques, over 70% of American families go to a shopping mall at least once a week, spending about $70 per person each time. The most intense "shop-'til-you-drop" compulsion is apparently found among Californians, who visit a shopping center 10.3 times in a three-month period. Teens between 14 and 17 make the highest number of mall trips per quarter at 13, and spend an average of 83.6 minutes there, mostly browsing.[12] It is, of course, not necessary to assume that people are seduced into these behavior patterns by the hoopla. Rather, to make sense of what they see and hear around them in the consumerspace, people naturally move "into the market." That's when their reaction to the advertising and promotion involves excitement and fun, as opposed to boredom and anger. If you can't fight 'em, join 'em.

From Consumer to Citizen

All or most consumers, not just anti-marketers, will at some time find themselves lamenting the onset of the materialism and commercialism that accompany unfettered brand competition. The new reality is likely to be seen as an attack on traditions and culture. Your "way of life" is challenged, as materialism takes up an increasing amount of living space and time, and non-commercial activities are forced to a backseat. This is not simply a matter of

---

12. These data come from *American Demographics*, September 01, 2003, p. 7.

individual priorities, but of everybody's daily life. As products proliferate, branding promotions multiply, markets are deregulated, and government services are privatized, individuals will spend a gradually greater share of their lives making decisions about matters previously not even thought about. Where before people could select among a limited number of well-established alternatives—and sometimes didn't even have a choice—they now have to accept responsibility for complex and difficult choices. It is hardly surprising if some of these people resent how their secure and comfortable lives are threatened.

Brand marketing fills our lives with transactions, materialism, and superficiality. According to statistics, shopping is the favored pastime of a majority of women in the U.S., and quite possibly others too. It is not surprising to find one recent book proclaiming that in the new era, consumers' lives center around "shopping and making love"—the latter activity expressed more succinctly—as if we were all young teenagers again. This might be a good recipe for a successful marriage, but ardor has its natural limits, and so does shopping.

 This is why marketing's efforts to spread materialism do seem to justify some of the charges against it. Material satisfaction is not the only goal of human activity. Marketers emphasize self-interested acquisition and make it the single most important factor: "You should buy this because it makes you feel good." In some ways, the new brand-building techniques become the "voice of vice." The seven vices are not exactly nurtured, but some quite aptly describe what anti-marketers complain about: Lust, Sloth, Pride, Envy, Greed, Gluttony, and Anger. There are clear reflections of these categories in the *Affluenza* program, Schlosser's *Fast Food Nation* book, and Quartz's *Branded* depiction of teenager influences.

The slightly unseemly undercurrent was less of a problem as long as the marketing was focused on the market exchange, product for money. But when the marketers started to communicate in terms of brand meaning, identity, and trust, they took on a different role from that of traditional marketers. Instead of a "neutral" provider, the marketer attempted to become a "favored friend" of the customer. The marketer replaced and substituted for other relationships, developing bonds that created pseudo-trust and provided meaning and identity. These are lofty objectives, and one cannot help feeling cynical about the effort, since the underlying premise is still bottom-line profitability. The relationship aimed for by marketers is one where the new intimacy is simply added to the old arsenal of persuasive tactics. Who hasn't been asked to complete a customer satisfaction questionnaire and heard the old saw: "If you cannot rate me 'Excellent,' give me the reason and I will fix it." As relationships go, this is not authentic. It is just old-fashioned sales jargon.

The New Brief

What it comes down to is that the case for anti-marketing is not simply based on the notion that the marketing of unsafe and unhealthy products should be regulated and perhaps prohibited. The new case for anti-marketing involves a much broader attack on the free market and its marketers. One main charge of the new anti-marketing involves the way marketing has made our lives so dominated by materialism. For example, the rate of technological innovation is so high that products are obsolete while still perfectly functional. The result is dissatisfaction with one's current possessions, a desire for the new versions, wastefulness, and the kind of preoccupation with consumption that *Affluenza* described. Another charge is that advances in communication technology enable marketers to reach us everywhere and all the time, making it difficult to avoid marketing pressure to consume. The media messages presume that we are always "in the market," and when most of the time we are not, they force us to shut down the communication channels or make quick decisions based on scant information.

Then there is the argument that competition has driven companies to imitate products and that instead of true functional differentiation, the available choices only differ in terms of brand image and identity. Loyalty to a brand can no longer be a function of uniqueness and special features, but of affinity and identification with the brand and what it stands for. The brands are the heroes that we emulate. Most anti-marketing commentators are averse to the way brands have taken over this role, whether in the case of teenagers or grizzled Harley-Davidson veterans.

The new anti-marketing case is basically against the dangers and excesses of the free market system. As I see it, the anti-marketers are not against the free market as such. Even anti-marketers recognize that making hospitals more responsive to patients can be good. Even they realize that getting new products is beneficial. New media such as the Internet do offer new opportunities. Experiential marketing usually involves more fun and exciting advertising than straight explanations of functional differences among products. There are economic efficiencies to large-scale production that translate to lower prices—and so on. But, the anti-marketers today argue that the process has gone too far, the system is out of whack, and our consumer paradise has turned into a quagmire of commercialism, consumption, and materialism. Marketing, they say, is a major culprit.

3 WHY DO MARKETERS DO WHAT THEY DO?

Is marketing ethical?

There are many people around the world—and in the U.S. as well—who wonder how marketers can do what they do without feeling sick to their stomachs. It is the same feeling I get when I read about the tobacco companies and the managers who work for them. How can they face their children? Their spouses? Even themselves in the mirror?

My own solution has always been to believe in the product I am selling. If you can convince yourself that the product or service you are selling yields positive benefits to the customer, that it's "good" in the sense that the customer will be better off for having bought it, then you are doing something good. A good product is by itself not enough, of course. In-your-face marketing involves tactics that can appall and affront people, regardless of the essential goodness of the product. But, a starting point for "ethical" marketing must be that the product is good. I teach this to my MBA students, and have had some of them (though not all) quit companies like Philip Morris for that reason. Other students, of course, do not even consider working for some of the companies disparaged for similar reasons.

Whether or not a product yields positive benefits can of course be a tricky question, especially since in many advanced markets, the needs satisfied are typically not very basic. I mean, we are not usually talking about feeding the poor and hungry or offering a drink to the thirsty masses. Marketers tend to make use of a theory of needs that is hierarchical, meaning that once basic survival needs are satisfied, there are higher order needs—the need for recognition, for achievement, for belonging, and so on—which also have to be satisfied for a person to be happy. A product that makes a person feel good is therefore also a "good" product to sell. While marketers prefer to speak of "satisfaction" instead of "happiness," there is always at least an implicit assumption that products and services will bring happiness to a person's life. This assumption is the source of the materialistic and commercialization dynamic of marketing. "We bring good things to life" as the General Electric slogan goes.

In-Your-Face Logic

The in-your-face marketing efforts discussed here, however, go way beyond the question of the goodness of the product. In fact, in many cases, the product itself is only tangentially involved in the effort. This is because to a marketer, perception is everything. A high-speed computer is a high-speed computer only if the customer thinks it is a high-speed computer. Think about it for a second and you'll see how it works. Take a car, for example. How do you judge if the car is fast or not? Figures seem to tell the story— "0–60 in 8 seconds"—but most people don't know how to read the numbers. "Sportiness" is the typical attribute automakers use, and this comes from styling, something everyone can judge. Now take a more mundane product like a bar of soap. How soft is it on the skin? According to market research, most people apparently use perfume strength to assess softness. Anyone can smell the soap. How about food and drink? Well, we know that people can tell beers apart when tasting—but only if they are allowed to see the bottles (although Guinness stout is an exception). As for food, there is not much scientific evidence that I have seen, but think about the effect on people when you tell them sushi is raw fish, or that chicken breast is actually rabbit meat. I make my students squirm in their seats when I tell them Swedes are very fond of smoked horsemeat. I doubt the same reaction would occur if they tasted it and were simply told it was smoked venison. Perception might not be everything, but it's small wonder if for marketers it seems more important than the product itself.

This is why the marketing efforts discussed in this book go far beyond the product. They also involve the design, the color, the brand name, the logo, and the whole marketing communications apparatus. In fact, the in-your-face marketing effort that affronts me most is the repetitive advertising slogans and noisy commercials I see on TV and hear on the radio. It's not easy to illustrate this on the written page, but we all have our favorite offenders. For me, the worst are the loud and abrasive TV commercials (with lots of sex, confrontation, and "attitude") my teenage daughters see, but then I am not in that market, so those shouldn't really count (I do tell them, however, to please watch something else). But how about those inane car commercials about zero financing, the insipid beer commercials touting sentimental patriotism, and Bob Dole hawking Viagra? Talk about a product to believe in—at least he is a person one can empathize with.

Promotional tactics

A few features make for the in-your-face character of many of these commercials. As you may have noticed already, when the commercials on TV come on, the volume automatically increases slightly. This is to catch your attention. The same intent is behind the quick editing and striking images that typically are used to pull you into the commercial's story. This can involve sex and violence, as we all know. Sometimes, the beginning trades on what is called "fear appeal," as when the tires of a car slip on a wet road, with a young mother driving and a baby in a baby-seat. Sex, violence, fear, and guilt are always assumed to be reliable motivators, used as glue to hook you to the screen. Not surprisingly, to choose between alternative cuts and edits of a commercial, ad agencies sometimes use tools such as pupil dilation measures, eye movement cameras, and "galvanic skin response," electrodes to monitor sweaty palms.

Having established "the problem," the story usually moves into a more rational mode, explaining why the advertised brand might in fact help solve the problem better than any of the competing brands on the market. These kinds of problem-solving commercials are staples of brands from many packaged goods manufacturers and are really not that objectionable, except when they try to get low-involvement products to seem very important for your emotional well-being. If you are "in the market" for some of these mundane products, getting some comparative evaluation of battery life, absorptive capacity of paper towels, or why a particular toothpaste fights cavities better than all the others, no real harm is done. If you are not in the market, you can just tune out—like we all do.

A lot of the in-your-face advertising really has little or no problem-solving purpose at a functional level. Rather, it plays on insecurity and inexperience, as well as a desire for status and other higher order needs to create emotional tensions (emotional "problems," if you will) that can then be cured by choosing the right brand. The situations often involve individual aspirations and social pressure. The commercials depict the dejection that comes from the disapproval of some significant other, and the subsequent catharsis that choosing the right brand will yield. Contrary to what you might suppose, this is not a simple logic that applies only to teenagers, but is at work in all segments of the market—and with all kinds of products and services. These kinds of emotional appeals are used for personal care products and apparel most decidedly, but also in ads for household products (the "good mother" image of Pampers), for major purchases such as computers and automobiles, and even in business-to-business markets (the way IBM and FedEx play on their recognition factor, for example). The right choice of brand will ease the tension, satisfy the customer, and fill a need, albeit a higher order one, awakened by the promotion. We might think we are immune to such obvious "tricks," but research consistently shows that such denials are empty gestures. For example, back in the 1970s when generic brands first appeared in the stores, even the black and white "Beer" cans turned out to have their own special cachet. My older daughter's Army surplus shirt makes its own statement. People are social animals.

In-your-face promotion also, of course, includes all that repetitive advertising that we see and hear, impressing brands and their slogans on everybody's mind. We all know the way jingles, logos, and spokespersons (or cartoons, or animals—take your pick) for certain products "help" us remember the appropriate brand name. It's Ronald McDonald, the Bud-wei-ser frogs, the "just-do-it" swoosh. These reminders are intended to be in your face quite literally, so that when the time comes to make a choice, you "naturally" and without thought reach for the embedded brand—or get upset if you can't find it on the shelf. In the beginning, marketers thought that these repetitive messages would be useful only for the first three occasions or so (after which a fatigue factor would reduce the effect to nil or negative), and then only for low-involvement, impulse-style products, where choices become almost instinctive. These research findings might still be valid in some countries, but the clutter of commercial messages in the U.S. has grown so dense that marketers have apparently decided to keep the barrage going for most kinds of products. The reason is simply that as the noise has grown, we have become increasingly desensitized, losing the use of our senses the way hard-rock fans lose their hearing. This is why in-your-face promotions sometimes seem akin to a frustrated parent shouting at his or her multitasking offspring: "Listen to me!"

The Marketer's View of People

Sometimes when I see TV commercials, I wonder what the marketers really think of people. They must think we are imbeciles or something. Where do they get this idea? It usually does not take me long to decipher the answer. After all, some of the research that we present to our students in the classroom gives a pretty good idea about how we in marketing view people. I know many of you might think that all the lip service to "our customers are the most important people" is bunk, but really, marketers do think that customers are important. It's just that we don't think our customers are really that smart.

I don't say that we marketers are any smarter, but the way it works is that when a marketer looks at all the research evidence about how consumers behave, it is difficult not to start thinking that people really are pretty incoherent shoppers. I should say right away that the reasons for this have more to do with the time and effort we spend on evaluating products and services than with any innate level of intelligence. Even the most educated and intelligent individual is capable of being influenced willy-nilly by some clever promotion and of making the most atrocious purchase decisions. I think you know what I mean; we all let our guard down at times. We buy useless things because they are on sale; we buy "American-made" only to find out the goods were made in China; or, we order a high-tech mosquito killer after seeing it advertised on TV, forgetting that we don't have electricity in the backyard. One of my esteemed colleagues stocked up on cases of French champagne as an investment, not realizing that the fizz dissipates over time.

Marketers do scientific research to back up such anecdotal evidence. Some of it is elegant and simple, as when two random samples of homemakers were shown a shopping list that differed only by one item. One list included "Maxwell House coffee," while the other list had "Nescafe instant coffee." When asked to describe the housewife with such a shopping list, the two samples differed significantly, with those shown the second list imagining a careless and irresponsible housewife. This was despite the fact that prior personal interviews had revealed no negative attitude toward instant coffee.[1] Another small test involved lining the pockets of identical overcoats with different materials and asking people to compare them. Invariably, pockets lined with softer material scored higher quality ratings. You have probably heard about the various blind tests of soft drinks, beer, and various snacks. Even devoted Coca-Cola drinkers, who forced the com-

---

Mason Haire, "Projective Techniques in Marketing Research," *Journal of Marketing*, April 1950, pp. 649–56.

pany to get back to "Classic" Coke, had not realized that the cola formula had been changed several times during their lifetime, but without announcements or packaging changes.[2] Without the logos available to view, there have apparently even been cases where colas and non-colas could not be reliably distinguished.[3] It sure is hard sometimes to take people's opinions seriously.

A lot of market research involves sophisticated design and large-scale data collection. Branding research, for example, which tries to assess the value of various brands, involves large surveys of respondents queried about a wide variety of brands. Research for new products can involve sophisticated analyses of consumers' responses to alternative designs, projecting laboratory test results to a forecast of market shares. Alternative promotional tools—things like coupons versus in-store cents-off, special aisle displays, or free home samples—are evaluated through computer-based analyses of massive sets of supermarket scanner data. For many of us marketers, these kinds of sophisticated scientific endeavors help to shield us from the realization that we are, in fact, evaluating means for manipulating people.

The empowered consumer?

Since the arrival of one-to-one marketing, the Internet, and relationship marketing, there has been much talk about the emergence of the empowered consumer. Marketers can no longer dictate what consumers should buy and use. Consumers are in control of the communications with any seller, expressing preferences, evaluating alternative prototypes, and even designing their own products, from cars and computers to shirts and shoes.

This glowing picture is correct as far as it goes. But because of the huge number of products and the massive communication efforts to sell them, consumers have little time to spend on any one single product or brand—unless, of course, shopping is all they do.

---

2. Patricia Winters, "For New Coke, 'What Price Success?'" *Advertising Age*, March 20, 1989, p. S-1, 2.

3. I heard this asserted once in an academic conference, but I have not yet seen it documented scientifically. As a consumer of soft drinks I find it hard to believe, but then, that's exactly the point—as consumers we are not as smart as we think.

Not surprisingly, while most consumers do spend at least some time on products or services that hold a particular interest—your tennis and golf, my classical music and opera, someone else's vintage cars and motorcycles—our empowerment to find out more about mortgage refinancing, cholesterol levels in salad dressings, and the energy efficiency of electric cars goes unheeded. There is just too much.

The sheer volume of products and services, coupled with their ever shorter lifecycles and the accompanying promotional noise, would lead one to suspect that consumers in the U.S. are less in control of things than before. I am not aware of any definite research to document this, and I am not sure consumers themselves would agree. I can hear my daughters' protests when I suggest that they are influenced by advertising. But we marketers know better—and the most recent research suggests that things are even worse than before.

In August 2003, a colleague and I went to the American Marketing Association meetings in Chicago to interview potential candidates for a position as an assistant professor at Georgetown. Hiring in the academic profession involves personal interviews with candidates, and a conference is a natural occasion since people gather from all over the world to attend. The interview tends to focus on the research that the candidate is doing for his or her doctoral dissertation. The topics naturally reflect the current trends in the profession. I expected to hear a lot about the "empowered" consumer from the 29 candidates we were scheduled to interview over the three-day period. I heard a lot of the opposite.

Before I talk about some of the candidates' research, please let me emphasize that this is clearly not a random sample of research in marketing. What companies do is in some ways different, since their research has more of a "bottom line" profitability orientation than academic research. Also, our 29 candidates were not randomly selected—we wanted someone who would teach our courses, but would also fit Georgetown's general research thrust into international, public policy, and ethics topics. But, the 29 were the best candidates from the best universities across this country and elsewhere. We interviewed doctoral students from

Columbia and Wharton, from UCLA and Stanford, from North-western, Florida, Michigan, and INSEAD, a leading business school in France.

State of the art

Of the 29 cases, no less than 22 did research on some aspect of what we call "consumer behavior," investigating the psychological and sociological factors that underlie a consumer's way of dealing with the marketplace of today. Three focused on how people deal with risky choices, a traditional topic confirming that women still tend to take less risks than men. Another three studied customer satisfaction—another traditional topic—one study showing how satisfaction can be influenced (manipulated?) by information and events that recalibrate expectations downward (one possibility is to simply wait with delivery of a product so that the immediate post-purchase euphoria can be given time to die down—Amazon.com covered that angle, it would seem). No less than seven studies focused on the role of emotion or "affect" in brand choice. The emotional attachment to a brand is by now a "given" in marketing, and the question is more how to create and nurse it. One candidate discussed his study of how emotional attachment can exacerbate any failure of a favorite brand—people really feel cheated.[4] Can the warm aura of sincerity around your brand get too hot? There is also clear evidence that people eat more when feeling down. More popcorn is consumed when watching sad movies than happy movies—although the viewers themselves don't seem to recognize this.[5]

I thought I would see some study of how people have now taken charge of their own consumer destiny. I guess I was biased, but honestly, there was very little of that. Instead, there were a cou-

---

4. This study was already accepted for publication. See Jennifer Aaker, Susan Fournier, and S. Adam Brasel. "When Good Brands Do Bad," *Journal of Consumer Research*, forthcoming, June 2004.

5. By Nitika Garg, University of Pittsburgh. Quoted with permission. The research is reported in Nitika Garg, Brian Wansink, and J. Jeffrey Inman, "The Influence of Incidental Affect on Consumer's Food Intake," working paper, 2004.

ple of studies of how incidental information about unrelated product categories (the Internet banner ads that suddenly pop up, for example) can influence choice, how the order of presentation (what is called *framing* in psychology) influences people's judgments, and how a large number of choices lowers people's confidence in making the best choice.[6] There was also a study of how people cope with consumer stress, something that would be useful for us here, but the study area is still in its infancy. The preliminary findings are that people who think themselves capable will do something about the stress; others will simply avoid facing the problem.[7]

One of the nails in the coffin for the "empowered" consumer came from a study of rebate redemption rates.[8] Rebates are particularly popular promotional tools used by technology retailers—cell phone marketing is a case in point—but they are also popular for packaged goods, where they are the number two tool after coupons. Redemption rates vary, but are generally low—less than 50% for big-ticket technology goods, and as low as 2% for packaged goods. Conventional wisdom would suggest that the redemption rate would increase as the dollar amount of the rebate goes higher since the gains are greater. The rate should also increase with the length of the redemption period, since the consumer has more time to submit the paperwork. The study did not support this conventional wisdom. The *purchase* rate increased, that is, more people bought when the amount and length of the period increased. But the *redemption* rate was largely not affected by the amount

---

6. By S. Adam Brasel, Stanford University. Quoted with permission. The research is reported in S. Adam Brasel, "Overwhelming Alternatives," working paper, 2004. The economists' notion that more choice is better is now under serious challenge from psychologists. See, e.g., Barry Schwartz, *The Paradox of Choice: Why More Is Less* (New York: Ecco), 2004.

7. By Adam Duhachek, Northwestern University. Quoted with permission. The research is reported in Adam Duhachek, "A Multidimensional Hierarchical Model of Coping: Examining Cognitive and Emotional Antecedents and Consequences," forthcoming, *Journal of Consumer Research*, 2004.

8. By Tim Silk, University of Florida. Quoted with permission. The research is reported in Tim Silk, "Why Do We Buy but Fail to Redeem? Influencing Consumers' Subjective and Objective Probability of Redeeming Mail-in Rebates," doctoral dissertation, University of Florida, 2004.

offered, and by extending the time limit, redemption rates actually decreased. This leads one to believe that when people are given plenty of time to do something, it never gets done. Advice for companies: Offer big rebates and give people a lot of time to redeem. You sell more, and it costs less.

To me, the most disconcerting study was one that tested whether ads work when people are warned of the persuasive intent (such as reminding people that the Marlboro cowboy is only trying to sell cigarettes).[9] In this study people were shown an advertisement for a shampoo, the ad coupled with the picture of a beautiful beach. The typical "creative" idea is that the beautiful beach would make people feel good about the shampoo brand. The study tried to stop the formation of this association by asking subjects to remember that the advertiser was only trying to sell shampoo. The well-established "Elaboration Likelihood Model" suggests that conscious reasoning should counter this kind of weak persuasive effort. However, the study found precisely the opposite: the association became stronger when subjects were asked to explicitly argue against the ad's influence. Subjects could not consciously stop the formation of a positive attitude toward the brand. The more we argue against something, the more we like it?

This finding also weakens the comfort of the thought that consumers are on to what marketers do. Research suggests that consumers do understand the "persuasion schemas" that marketers employ, that there is a certain sequence of tactics employed to gain compliance from the consumer.[10] But if the persuasion works despite this consciousness, it is truly hard to defend yourself against marketers' influence.

I must emphasize that in no way do I wish to somehow indict these projects for their choice of topics. These are very valid aca-

---

9.   By Maria Galli of INSEAD, France. Quoted with permission. The research is reported in Maria Galli, Amitava Chattopadhyay, and C. Miguel Brendl, "Persuasion Via Associative Mechanisms: Are We In Control?," INSEAD working paper, 2004.

10. Marian Friestad and Peter Wright, "The Persuasion Knowledge Model—How People Cope With Persuasion Attempts," *Journal of Consumer Research*, Vol. 21, June 1994, pp. 1–31.

demic subjects and are equally useful on either side of any debate, pro or con consumers. I should also caution, again, that these are only "selections" of current academic research in marketing. Furthermore, most of the studies have not yet been subjected to the peer review necessary to pass muster in the profession. Nevertheless, the absence of optimistic pronouncements of a sovereign and empowered consumer was striking. There was little or no evidence that consumer paradise was here, that consumers were freer than ever. Rather, I came away with the feeling that consumerspace is a cage in which many of us are trapped. Yes, we have all the products and all the excitement we want and more, but we don't seem to cope very coherently with our situation. Are we the Osbournes?

Marketing know-how

For most real-world marketers, these new academic findings are still treated as just that, "academic." But, there are a few long-established market research findings that really resonate with most marketing practitioners and that I think help explain why marketers do what they do. They are the kinds of insights that constitute part of what is known as "marketing know-how," but some might call them "tricks of the trade." They reflect how marketers think of people. Here are five selections:

1. "Mere exposure"—Exposing an audience to a certain message and then repeating it over and over again tends to generate a positive change in attitude—not just an acceptance of the message, but a positive attitude toward it. For example, popular hit songs tend to be those that people are able to hear repeatedly over the airwaves. While the initial reaction to something new and unfamiliar may be negative, just hearing or seeing it repeatedly makes it more familiar and acceptable. Thus, the repetition of slogans: They may seem annoying, but the theory is that they become part of the familiar and thus comfortable environment. Bush's "staying on message" strategy when discussing Iraq is a good illustration of this principle. It is mere exposure.

2. "Luxury becomes necessity"—Once luxury is tasted, it becomes a necessity. Just as for Adam after Eve's apple, there is no return to Paradise. There is no going back; levels of aspirations will always rise as possessions increase. Materialism is unlikely to bring happiness on its own. It takes almost a religious conversion to swear off the never-ending spiral. "Affluenza" is a great example of how this works, and how it has affected Americans' willingness to work hard and take no vacations.

3. "Money is relative"—Beyond mere survival, relative income is what matters. It was an economist, James Duesenberry, who first argued that increasing prosperity will not necessarily lead to greater satisfaction. The key is improving one's lot vis-à-vis one's neighbor's. Not just "keeping up with the Jones's," but "beating the Jones's." When everybody else loses more in the stock market than you do, your relative wealth has gone up. The fact that we marketers bring good things to poor people is not enough. We also have to make sure the distribution is seen as fair, which presents a tough problem with free markets.

4. "New choices create headaches"—Becoming aware of new alternatives has the effect of making current possessions seem less valuable. Opening markets to new products and services will easily create tension and dissatisfaction. Knowing that you can have a Hummer will reduce the satisfaction level for many SUV owners. When a company introduces its brand in a foreign market, not only will domestic competitors be pressured, but so will many consumers.

5. "Foot in the door"—While a potential customer may be reluctant to commit to one major purchase, presenting a smaller and more affordable first sacrifice makes later incremental charges more acceptable. This is an example of a "You give them a hand, they'll take the arm" kind of thing. This is why the "Try it at home and return it if not satisfied" promotion works—few will return the goods. The entry of a McDonald's outlet in a new country might

seem a small and unremarkable step, but really, it takes on a much greater significance.

So, marketers do not have such an uplifting view of human nature. If they think that they have a good product to sell—a judgment perhaps based on market test results—they see nothing wrong with trying to tell prospective customers about it. The objections—people don't want to hear about it, they are already satisfied with existing products, there is little need for the new product—are ignored. Taking such an objection to "innovation" seriously would not only stop the enterprise—and the economy—in its tracks, people do not really know what they want anyway. So, marketers tend to use an in-your-face approach to get your attention, to point to a problem that you did not know you had, to present their product's alleged benefits, and to repeat the brand name enough times so that it is embedded in your consciousness.

Competitive Pressure

Regardless of how benign or cynical a marketer's view of people is, the intensity of competitive rivalry in open and free markets will frequently be a dominating factor in strategic and tactical marketing decision-making. One can even say that a lot of the in-your-face efforts come from marketers set on dominating competitors, and going over the top in their effort.

In a sense, competition has always been a factor as long as marketing has been around, in fact as long as business has been around. After all, the key ingredient in a successful business is to provide a differentiating benefit, something that the competition cannot offer, something that generates a sustainable competitive advantage. One reason why the in-your-face efforts in marketing have risen to new heights is simply that the intensity of competition has grown apace with the globalization of markets.

Partly it is a question of numbers. Open and free markets entice new entrants who help raise the promotional intensity in an industry. Having more advertisers means having more advertising. But, perhaps what matters more is the fact that the competitive battle has shifted from product differentiation to less tangible attributes such as brand image and style. The rapid diffusion of technology and rejection of the "not invented here" syndrome have helped many companies incorporate new features from competitors into their own products, obliterating their competitors' advantages. This is why consumer choices in advanced countries depend so much on price and promotion, forcing companies to go to ever greater efforts to hype their offerings.

This was neither an obvious nor easily predictable result from globalization. There was no real reason to expect companies' products to become more alike. It was the emergence of best practices, reverse-engineering, and imitative design that led to a greater importance of promotion. The shift in thinking was mostly due to the Japanese companies' success with imitative product design strategies. As we will see later, the Japanese preference to not necessarily bring new products and new features to the marketplace, but to improve versions of the existing market leaders, is one explanation why their approach overseas seemed so much better attuned to the local conditions than the American way of doing it.

It is not surprising that the shift to communications and promotions as differentiation devices also has meant more and louder promotional efforts than before. Since functional differences between products are relatively minor, promotion of brand and image is the only way to avoid debilitating price competition. If one competitor tries to lower the pressure, other competitors will gain. Many companies advertise heavily to at least match their competition, not really being able to gauge the effectiveness (or lack of it) of the effort. Increasing the stridency and the amount of the effort serves to attract the attention of the prospects and dominate competitors. Then, if people behave as marketers suppose, there is a chance to convert a prospect to a customer. All in all, it is not a pretty scenario.

Marketing as warfare

The marketing activities that many of us are most familiar with are not so obviously based on the idea of satisfying our needs and preferences. This is because the markets in many developed countries are basically mature, even saturated. Marketing involves as much the creation of needs and wants as the satisfaction of them. Actually, marketing often has to start with the creation of dissatisfaction, making you displeased with the state of your present possessions. Only then will you be open to information about "new and improved" options. Marketers frequently compare marketing to warfare, with branding strategies conceived as an attack on a competitor's stronghold rather than simply satisfying customer needs.

The idea of marketing as warfare has a fairly long history, and does crop up now and then in most academic texts on marketing management. In 1986, a book entitled *Marketing Warfare* was published by two well-known advertising consultants, Al Ries and Jack Trout. They applied the military strategy principles of von Clausewitz to marketing strategy. Strikingly, comparing marketing efforts to military action means that competitors are the enemy, while consumers become the battlefield. As the authors proclaim at the outset: "The true nature of marketing today is not serving the customer; it is outwitting, outflanking, outfighting your competition. In short, marketing is war where the enemy is the competition and the customer is the ground to be won."[11]

For all its assumed "empowerment" of the consumer, the Internet go-go years of the 1990s did not diminish the relevance of this analogy. As the Preface to the 1998 reprint of the book states: "A decade ago, the term 'global economy' didn't exist....Today's marketplace makes the one we wrote about look like a tea party. The wars are escalating and breaking out in every part of the globe....All this means that the principles of *Marketing Warfare* are more important than ever."[12]

Albeit one should not take such promotional hyperbole at face value; such language is regrettable. However, the point about military strategic thinking being part and parcel of marketing

---

11. Al Ries and Jack Trout. *Marketing Warfare* (New York: McGraw-Hill), 1986, p. vi.

12. Ibid.

remains. For example, it is easy to relate the emphasis of von Clausewitz (and current American military doctrine) on the use of dominant force directly to the consolidation of businesses and the concentration of marketing spending behind a few global power brands. Big beats small.

Today's emphasis on the importance of the brand has not diminished the war-type rhetoric used by marketers—quite the contrary. Other contributing factors of course might be the political and military situations in the country, although it really seems farfetched to ascribe any direct effect from the Iraq war. In any case, a reasonable person might well shudder reading the titles of the current crop of branding business books: *How to Build a Killer Brand, Differentiate or Die: Survival in the Era of Killer Competition, Warp-speed Branding, Only the Paranoid Survive*. These are not very encouraging metaphors.

Damned If You Do...

The upshot of the marketer's view of people, the need to make a profit, and the current competitive climate is that there seem to be few options to using strong promotional tools. The marketer has an arsenal of weapons by which a potential customer's objections or reluctance may be overcome. These tools are by no means perfect and never-failing. In fact, it takes a great deal of cultural fine-tuning to generate just the right kind of sales message—and then the effort may prove futile anyway. What *is* important, however, is that the marketer is always in a selling mode and that there are tools that can be—and are—used to persuade the prospect. As we say in our marketing classes: As marketers, we must make sure that we are selling products we believe in, products that can improve the buyers' lives. Trust me?

For non-Americans, the price they pay for opening their markets is higher than it seems to Americans. They will be inundated with strident efforts from entrants without the national legitimacy or cultural understanding to convince them to improve their lot by buying new products and brands, to get rid of their old possessions. The benefits they get are not as great as for the Americans, since many of the products are not adapted to their specific culture or environment. The chance to arrive at a higher standard of living is compromised by a new focus on material possessions and economic comparisons, while leaving less room for past attention to local culture. On top of that, given the age-old conflicts between neighbors of different ethnicities in the old countries, one should not be surprised to find that the new wealth, unevenly distributed, helps to exacerbate already tense relationships. Avoiding conspicuous consumption might still be feasible in a country such as the U.S. where everyone is told from childhood that they can succeed. It is a less likely possibility in countries with zero-sum situations of one player gets all, the rest nothing, and envy of your neighbor is a dominant cultural trait. The new products and brands become weapons in age-old rivalries in these countries, so that the freer and more open marketplace creates rather than overcomes frustrations. Channeling such frustrations into an anti-global attitude is just a short step away.

CHAPTER

4 GLOBAL MARKETING AS BAD MARKETING

Selling it like it is

The "good marketing" idea has always been that marketers serve customers, not the other way around. Corporations operating with a customer orientation do not simply sell what they make, but make what they can sell. The products manufactured are those that prior research shows customers want. Of course, it is not such a simple thing for customers to tell you exactly what they want until the product is available to them. In saturated markets especially, we consumers want it when we see it, not before. Still, companies gather focus groups of potential consumers to evaluate new designs, ask consumers to trade off features ("Do you want longer battery life if it means a heavier unit?" types of questions), launch prototypes in selected test market areas, and so on before committing to a new product. It's an imperfect science, but in many companies, there is a sincere effort to divine what customers want before market rollout.

As a rule, this is not true in global marketing, even for companies that subscribe to these principles. The typical marketer going abroad aims to sell his or her product, not ask what people want. Sure, there will be some preliminary assessment of market potential, but rarely will a new product be contemplated. There are exceptions, and we'll come to those. But by and large, global marketers sell what they make. They have what is called a "sales orientation" as opposed to a true "mar-

keting orientation." Compared to domestic makers, they have the added burden of explaining to consumers why their products should be preferred, since most of them have not been tested in those markets. And they are foreign as well. Of course, if the foreign marketer assumes that he or she is coming as the savior of the downtrodden poor, these things don't really matter. Since this product was good enough at home, it should be good enough here. Or, in marketing terms, since the product has been successful in a leading market, it should be launched in follower markets. It is not surprising that some of these new entries into the local marketplace have stirred up resentment and anti-globalization sentiment among some local consumers.

A Sales Orientation

The sales orientation is not really a sign of arrogance. It is, in a sense, unavoidable. A completely new product is difficult to introduce successfully in any market. Doing it in a foreign market only adds to the problems. The distance and the foreignness mean that customers are not easily understood, that distribution channels are strange, and that competitors are different. Differences in language and culture make for new ways of doing business. All of this means that the marketer can typically consider entry into a new market abroad only after a given product is successful elsewhere, usually at home.

First off, you've got to have something to sell. Global marketing typically involves pushing an existing product into a new market. It's like trying to move customer preferences toward your brand rather than adapting the brand to where the market is. In some ways, one should be surprised when consumer sympathies actually do shift, as when Budweiser and Corona beers score any sales in Germany, at least temporarily.

To be sure, there are cases where a global marketer, after assessing the preferences in a foreign market, has introduced completely new products there. The Japanese have several examples of this. Toshiba, the first to introduce the laptop computer, designed it for the American market. Sony's sporty Walkman designs are targeted at the rougher boys in the West. The Japanese luxury cars—Acura by Honda, Lexus by Toyota, and Infiniti by Nissan—were not only designed for Western markets, they were also given new brand names and dealerships. Western, and even American, companies have also done this. Procter & Gamble, the large manufacturer of household and personal care products, has a European product line that differs from that at home in the U.S.

Some companies today develop products and services with an eye to introducing them into the global market directly, attempting to satisfy everyone through one design. This is usually done with the help of a so-called *platform design*, a base on which several versions of the final model can be mounted. This kind of modular design is followed in cameras, computers, autos, even in services such as hotels and banking. It allows the "bells and whistles" of the final offering to be customized to different target groups and countries.

From a marketing viewpoint, these are the exceptions. The brands of the products and services discussed in this book—the Nikes, the Starbucks, the McDonald's, the Coca-Colas, the Wal-Marts, and so on—basically involve existing brands in pretty much unadulterated form expanding outward from their home country. The global marketer's task is basically to figure out what kind of distribution organization to set up, how fast the rollout should be, what the introductory promotional campaign should involve (and how much it should cost), and how to track the rate of market penetration. These are not small tasks, especially considering that they must be done for every country and market involved. To start thinking about new products on top of that is not only making things more complicated, it will increase costs sharply.

Global standardization

Even existing products and services can be adapted. This was the typical marketing solution in the era of multinationals, before globalization took hold. One standard pattern for American and European multinationals was to manage an international division independently of the home country, reaching abroad through country subsidiaries run by strong local managers, plus some expatriate at the top for control purposes. The local subsidiaries could draw on the product lines of the company, choosing the models and versions which best fit their market, and adapting the products and marketing program to their local customers, even developing their own products. For example, both Ford and GM run strong operations in Europe with cars designed primarily for the European market.

During the globalization of the last two decades, this has changed. The turning point occurred with a famous 1983 *Harvard Business Review* article by Ted Levitt, which proclaimed that in the new global era, multinationalism was giving way to global homogeneity.[1] The premise was that people everywhere want the same thing. The stage was set for globally standardized products, which, because of scale and scope economies, would let companies provide products with state-of-the-art technology at low cost.

As we will come back to later, this simple globalization notion has recently been countered by a rise in pro-domestic sentiments, which is forcing companies to more local customization. But, with a few exceptions, this is a very new development of the past couple of years, and not many global companies have been able to respond effectively yet. Also, it is not clear that all these global companies take the localization trend seriously yet, given that it is so recent. As a result, for most global companies, there are still limits to which existing products and services have been adapted to local tastes and requirements. This holds true also for advertising, pricing, and other elements of the marketing mix. In addition, the use of IMC necessarily constrains the freedom of local subsidiaries to develop their own campaigns.

In advertising, using state-of-the-art technology and film directors, global TV commercials are shot in extravagant surroundings and at extraordinary expense, recuperated only because they can be shown around the world. Shifting dialogue from speaking

1.   Ted Levitt, "The Globalization of Markets," *Harvard Business Review*, May–June, 1983, pp. 92-102.

actors to voice-overs, which can be dubbed into different lan-
guages more easily, and finally to music-only with unintelligible
words if necessary, allows the audio portion of commercials to be
unchanged. As for the video portion, to cut costs further, some
ideal "guy" or "gal" can be used. (Perhaps not surprisingly, one
favored country in which these models are found is Australia,
where the heritage of mixed races has produced such archetypes,
as film-makers have discovered.)

Needless to say, standardization affects people's behavior, habits,
and tastes. When Starbucks offers coffee in large paper mugs,
people have to get used to it. When TV commercials use the latest
in digital technology, people will start to expect such wizardry in
competitors' shots. When package sizes are bigger than before,
shopping habits have to change. The degree to which such
changes are acceptable differs of course between groups in the
population. With the high level of "noise" created by the saturation campaigns, the "mere exposure" effect can change people's
thinking about what is normal. This helps to explain why people
now drink coffee and talk on the phone when they drive, why
paying by cash takes more time than paying by credit card, and
so on. Levitt's 1983 thesis about standardization as the wave of
the future might have seemed ahead of its time, but the marketing efforts of global companies have helped it come true. They
have also, as we have seen, helped to create the anti-globalization
backlash and a return toward localization.

Global coordination

To reap the scale and scope benefits of global reach, the marketing effort has to be coordinated across countries. Product rollouts
in different countries need to be coordinated with production
capacity at central plants. Global advertising campaigns have to
break locally when products are made available across countries.
Training in customer service has to be finished by the time the
sales season starts in different countries. But this means that
what happens in one country's market depends on actions in
other countries. In the previous multinational era, the sheer complexity of this synchronization effort made companies treat country subsidiaries as free-standing profit centers, more or less

inadvertently making local adaptation natural. Many companies even became "native," the way the Norelco, Electrolux, and Nivea brands seem not to evoke their home countries (Holland, Sweden, and Germany, respectively).

For global companies, standardization can be seen as a prerequisite for effective coordination, since it is more difficult to coordinate across dissimilar products and marketing activities. The resulting interdependence will not always be perceived as a gain for local customers, who realize that what they are now offered depends on what other countries get.

Of course, in many cases, consumers won't know any of this, although they may suspect it. The delays in the Microsoft Windows '98 release were due to the difficulty of coordinating 30 language versions for simultaneous launch. Even though the company festivities accompanying the product's global launch were held as scheduled, and public announcements about the simultaneous launch were not retracted, the actual release dates depended on when sufficient resources were freed up from other launches. Thus, after the U.S. and European releases in mid-1998, the Chinese launch came on September 2, and the Thai version on October 28. And some countries did not get Windows '98 until '99.

Globalization is top-down

Finally, one reason for a deficient customer orientation is the decidedly centralized character of most firms' global marketing efforts. The marketing is directed from the company's home country. To implement global marketing policies, headquarters must reduce the local subsidiaries' authority. What those at headquarters decide will have to be followed abroad. Even under the best of circumstances, with cross-country product teams, strategic input from lead countries and global mandates for local subsidiaries, the global marketing effort must be a top-down activity.

For example, Disney's release dates for films and videos are set from its Orlando headquarters. The promotional use of the Nike swoosh, its color, size, and placement, is carefully monitored by Beaverton headquarters. Ford pulled back responsibility for design, engineering, and marketing from its subsidiary in Cologne, Germany to Dagenham, England, and then to Dearborn, Michigan. Centralization is not simply senior-level decision-making. Volvo cars did not feature mug holders until recently, despite appeals from its American dealers. Volvo engineers in Sweden were too busy with more serious design issues.

Nowhere is centralization more prominent than in the strategic use of brands. Today, the choice and use of brand names are typically tightly controlled from headquarters. Global companies, from Pepsico to Sony to Electrolux, have strict guidelines for how their brand name should appear, in what color and font, the size of the logo, and so on. The top also decides which brand names to promote globally, which regionally, which to retain nationally, and which to drop altogether. Because of the mergers and acquisitions made possible by deregulated financial markets, today's multinational companies, especially in the packaged products category, control a wide variety of brands. In the mid-1990s, Nestle, the Swiss multinational, owned a total of 560 brands, many local only. In its drive toward global power brands, the company has decided to put its promotional muscle behind a few large brands to the relative neglect of others. Thus, among its bottled water brands, Nestle has given Perrier global status, while Vittell is regional, and Ramlosa is national only. Some brands are dropped entirely or sold off. Well-known global brands are not only attractive targets for anti-globalization activists because of their newsworthiness, but also because they precisely represent the global organization.

Just like the standardization of products, centralization is necessary to accomplish the coordination required to pursue global markets. It has also come to mean that global companies tend to be more ethnocentric than the old-style multinationals. Not only are managers gathered in one location, but the necessary face-to-face interactions, although typically conducted in the English language, are based on a common understanding of the company and its roots. This common understanding facilitates the required coordination. At the same time, as always with centralization, the company begins to take on the character of the person or people at the top. The resulting organizational culture often reflects a very idiosyncratic version of the top people's national character, making it less transparent and more difficult for outsiders to penetrate.

This is why global companies, paradoxically, often exhibit strong ethnocentric characteristics (as do their brands, which are designed to encapsulate these characteristics). Nike, Levi's, and Coca-Cola are quintessentially American, with a free-swinging style. Mercedes, BMW, and Siemens are German, steady and methodical. Toyota, Panasonic, and Toshiba are essentially Japanese, very closed and conservative. Honda and Sony, two maverick Japanese companies, are more open, but even they have had to pull back: Honda from an attempt to establish three global headquarters (in U.S. and Europe in addition to Japan) and Sony from staffing its American subsidiary with Americans only.

To sum up, global marketing is not a model of "good marketing." It almost always has a selling orientation. It is opportunistic and basically tries to leverage existing resources in new markets, using standardization to gain cost efficiencies. It almost always involves the removal of a decision-making authority away from the market. It means less autonomy for local subsidiaries to better coordinate operations across countries. Decisions affecting local markets and employees are no longer made in the market country, but abroad. The foreign managers who make these decisions come from a different culture, with a particular tradition. They and their organizations are influenced by this tradition. American global firms reflect and embody some if not all American values, as do Japanese and European firms reflect their home countries' traditions. It doesn't take much imagination on the part of a local anti-globalization activist to infer that the new foreign brand in the local marketplace represents a neo-colonial power, especially if the country of origin is an avowed hegemon.

Foreign Country of Origin

The foreignness of the global marketer also helps explain the fact that, as much research shows, country of origin can matter a great deal when products and services are bought. Early on in the globalization process, marketers expected that country of origin would matter gradually less. After all, a multinational corporation might manufacture a product and its components in several different countries. But as it turns out, countries have special skills that companies exploit and enhance, and opinion leaders recognize. Italian styling, French perfume, Indian software: These are not empty labels; they indicate a certain level of competence and quality. Even if experts know to be more specific—northern Venice, in the south around Grasse, or in Bangalore, for example—for many consumers, the country names are sufficient. People buy, or don't buy, as the case might be, "French" wines, "German" beer, or "Japanese" cars. Whether or not used explicitly for marketing purposes, their validity reinforces the use of "Made in" and "Made by" labels to judge products and services.

It's not only where a *product* is made that matters, but so does where the *brand* comes from and where the headquarters of the maker are located. Global brands have definite home countries. According to market research, a Sony television set made in San Diego, California is still "Japanese." The brand name says by whom the product is made, and companies maintain quality wherever they produce, to protect the value of the brand name.

Thus, paradoxically, globalization has led to greater marketing importance for country borders than previously, when they mainly served as trade obstacles. Or, stated another way, as borders have lost their significance for distribution because of tariff reductions, the symbolic significance of country borders for brand management has increased. But this also has a drawback for marketers. It means that, except at home, the global marketer is a foreigner, not an insider in each market, as was once projected. And this in turn affects the legitimacy by which the marketer can claim "equal time" with the customers.

Legitimacy abroad

Beyond the question of whether the global marketer is sensitive to the local culture, or whether the country of origin has a positive image, there is also a question of the legitimacy of the marketing effort. Entering emerging markets where needs are clear, the marketer's role is usually unambiguous: provide needed new products and services at the least cost possible. In advanced markets, by contrast, the global marketer's primary task at entry is typically to break existing habits. The marketing effort focuses on persuasive tactics to convince consumers to switch to new brands. The legitimacy of an in-your-face approach is much greater when selling at home than when operating in a foreign country, in particular if the product or service is not adapted to the new market. Even with trade barriers reduced or eliminated, the firm is not a citizen in the new country's market, but a guest. To speak as if one were at home might backfire, not only among one's customers, but also in the society at large. Thus, when abroad a company cannot so easily dismiss complaints about intrusive commercialization, even when one's customers are satisfied and the complaints come from other citizens.

The question of legitimacy also affects the use of other marketing practices. As we saw in Chapter 2, recent "good marketing" techniques have emphasized the relationship-building aspects of a customer orientation. In relationship-building, the "new" marketing techniques involve positioning one's offering as a hand reaching out to help a "friend." Using such an approach in a foreign market is easily seen as simultaneously patronizing and preposterous. At home in a certain culture, such as in America, these efforts may seem acceptable, but even among Americans, such actions can lead to suspicion and cynicism, since the instrumentality of actions clearly dominates any genuine feelings. In a foreign culture, not only might the self-serving motive be an affront, but so might the implied equality. This is the American dilemma well-portrayed in the classic 1958 book *The Ugly American* by William Lederer and Eugene Burdick.[2] Americans like to poke fun at "The government is here to help you" slogan, but we would

---

2. William J. Lederer and Eugene Burdick, *The Ugly American* (New York: W.W.Norton), 1958. Ironically, of course, the ugly American of the title was a good guy—the "ugly" Americans were his more polished superiors.

do well to look at the way we marketers have adopted the same attitude with relationship marketing, with no sense of irony.

Foreign dominance

Despite all of these weaknesses, when markets open up, entering global brands will typically have definite competitive advantages over local brands. Partly this is a matter of selection—if they didn't have any competitive advantage, they would not enter. But, these advantages do not always or necessarily reside in functionally better products or services, and as we know, the entrants are not necessarily adapted to local conditions and demand preferences. Most often, the advantages are resource-based: brand strength, stronger financials, and cost efficiencies from global scale. The big fish eat the little fish.

The defense for the local brands will typically involve further adaptation to local tastes, a stress on the domestic origin of the brand, improved quality, more intensive distribution (through closer relationships with resellers, for example—hard to match for a foreigner), and the consolidation of several domestic producers to match the scale advantages. Where a single brand manages a strong defense through a loyal following, it may simply be bought by a global entrant. Thus, even if the number of brands stays the same or momentarily increases, the typical result of open markets will be fewer players. As these producers try to generate cost efficiencies and leverage assets, they will gradually weed out some brands, focus on the larger brands, and variety will diminish. Local markets in one country will become indistinguishable from other countries.

Why would this antagonize consumers? One part of the answer is that many lose their favorite brand, the way Coca-Cola drinkers lost "their" brand when New Coke came in. Another is that the reduction in locally adapted products lessens the special character of the native market, the way English pubs are forced to cut down on the number of dark beers sold in favor of Bud, Heineken, and others. This is the argument advanced by many anti-globalization sympathizers. A third is that the loss of local control makes attention to the local brand dependent on companies' successes and failures elsewhere, so that Ford's problems in the U.S. are reflected in the new product resources allocated to its Volvo subsidiary. And, the consolation of being part of the greater world and getting "world-class" products is less attractive when local companies close and people lose jobs.

Who needs foreign brands?

The recent localization movement has undoubtedly been stirred both by the anti-globalizers and by the insensitive market actions of global firms. These forces seem to have helped energize the local entrepreneurs and have helped to stall the further dominance of global brands. They have even helped local brands to venture outside of their home countries, a kind of globalization in reverse. But, the resurgence of localization has also, unfortunately, given fuel to a common misconception that speaks to a latent protectionist sentiment among some people: We don't need foreign brands or free trade.

There is no gainsaying the statistical fact that the standard of living is higher with free markets. In most developed countries, materially speaking, you live better with free markets. But at any point in time, with saturated markets, there seems to be no particular need for global products or brands per se. This means that many people will see little need for free trade as such. Many countries can be self-sufficient and provide the necessary range of products and brands needed to fill most of the population's needs. Of course, there may be a need to import some raw materials lacking in a country, but by and large, for the kinds of products and brands in focus here, it is hard to claim some kind of absolute need.

This is why in many advanced countries, there are people who claim they don't need foreign imports. I should emphasize that I am talking about developed countries. When we talk about how bad things are in closed markets, we often confuse experiences in Bangladesh, Myanmar, and Zimbabwe with what is happening in, say, Europe. In underdeveloped countries, the need for better foreign products is palpable. But, you can meet people in Japan and in Europe who voice their opinion that, "We don't need many

American products." Good examples might be Denmark and Norway, where conservative forces dominate and keep the countries out of the mainstream. This is pretty similar to the sentiment sometimes voiced in the U.S. about foreign products. From an economic perspective, such instincts are of course completely misguided.

To understand anti-globalization and attacks on foreign brands, it is important to realize how easily these ideas form. Please do the following thought experiment suggested to me by a German manager working for Ford in Cologne, Germany. Think about the typical products a family needs and see how a "German-only" family might fare:

- Appliances, white goods: German Bosch and Miele are as good as any
- Appliances, brown goods: Germany has Siemens, Telefunken, Braun, BASF
- Automobiles: How about BMW, Mercedes, Volkswagen?
- Computers: Nixdorff, Siemens
- Designer clothes: Hugo Boss
- Food and drink: Wurst and Kartoffelsalat, but also Beck's
- Personal care: Nivea
- Cleaning products: Henkel
- Pharmaceuticals: Bayer, Hoechst
- Financial services: Deutsche Bank
- Athletic shoes: adidas, Puma

This list can of course be extended, but the point is that a country such as Germany—and many other advanced countries—can do well without non-German brands, thank you, and will do very well if we simply allow European brands in the list. (The list only includes German brands.) The alternatives might be fewer than would be the case if the markets were open, especially in the TV entertainment category; one would expect a void without American programs—*The Simpsons* et al.

What does this prove? It simply shows that the need for the world's marketplace is not the kind of "must have" proposition that the pro-globalization forces seem to suggest. There is undoubtedly a desire for some global products and brands, especially among the young (Coca-Cola, Sony, McDonald's, Levi's, and MTV), but other than that, one can easily understand why commentators might question—as they routinely do in a country such as Japan—the need for markets to be open and free. The answer of course is in the greater economic good of large-scale economics and competition, the fruits of which over time will benefit each and every consumer. And it is shortsighted not to realize that if we want to export, we also need to import. But in the short run, if there are obvious sacrifices in terms of faster change, potential plant closures, and lost jobs, and increased uncertainty about the future, one can appreciate the reluctance of many to embrace the coming of the global marketers.

The U.S. Size (Dis-)Advantage

Many of the negative aspects of global marketing may seem academic to Americans. They are probably more obvious to non-Americans less attuned to the bustling, modern, in-your-face marketplace. The reason is not just more tolerance for noise among Americans, however. A more important reason is that the American market is large enough to economically justify local adaptation, and competitive enough to force it.

Many of the insensitivities of global marketing efforts are not as common in the American market as they are in other markets. America cannot be ignored; it's just too big. It is sufficiently large that scales of economy can be captured even though products are adapted specifically to U.S. market requirements. Most foreign entrants will adapt to American preferences, not needing to rely on standardization for cost efficiencies. The big crowds of people in shopping malls are good for business *and* consumers, however annoying.

In addition, the openness of the American marketplace makes it very competitive, and forces entrants to pay special attention to the market. For many non-American firms, the North American market is the largest single market, and success there becomes a first priority. This is why new products are developed specifically for American consumers, and design centers for foreign companies are as likely to be located in California as at home. The Toyota Celica is one example where American designers had a strong impact on the styling, and the same is true for the Toyota Camry and Honda Civic. The Ford Motor Company has gone the other way, using its European styling know-how to introduce the Taurus to American consumers, only to scale back its European-ness when Americans objected to the more extreme oval-shaped windows.

Other product categories where American preferences have forced adaptation in otherwise successful imports include JBL speakers (bigger bass woofers), Italian Nutella chocolate spread (larger containers), and IKEA's European king-sized beds (too narrow). As everybody seems to know, American RCA Victor also helped erase the early advantage of Betamax over the VHS video format, by insisting on enough recording time for NFL football games (3–4 hours), a challenge that Japan Victor, a subsidiary of Panasonic's Matsushita, was first to meet. The point is that Americans have an advantage in representing such a big market opportunity that global marketers can't neglect them. This is true even though in many cases, the differences in state laws and regulations make adaptation costly. To accommodate this, many importers opt for localization to the state with the most severe legislation; in many product categories, what America gets is actually what California wants.

In many smaller countries, people are not so lucky. The cost of adaptation precludes localization, and consumers have to accept that what they get is what is sold elsewhere, whether or not those markets are similar. Even if there is a German language version of Microsoft Office, it is not likely to be a Finnish one. The buyer of an American car in Great Britain will have to foot the bill for the requisite homologation requirements. When central Europeans take to Harlequin Romances, they will be able to read in their own language, but it will be some time before they get stories where the action is in recognizable places. The Coca-Cola, KFC, and Starbucks you get in foreign places will be close to the real thing, even though typically the sugar levels have been reduced, Americans being more fond of sugar than many other people.

Of course, this opens up a niche opportunity for smaller manufacturers, which can provide adapted products, but usually at higher prices. For travelers, these products can be eye-opening and pleasant discoveries. Some examples are: the deeper bathtubs of Europe compared with the shallow bathtubs of the U.S., which are designed for cost-efficient mass production; the beds of Germany, massive wooden structures that ship only at great expense to the markets where steel frames are *comme-il-faut*; the longevity of the well-stitched children's apparel in Japan compared with the rapid deterioration of comparable American wear—but then, Miki House clothes are much more expensive. Not all these niche efforts will of course be in much demand elsewhere regardless of price. For example, entrepreneurial publishers in Abidjan on the Ivory Coast use local writers to craft romance stories with African heroes and heroines—a big local success, but probably not a serious competitor to global powerhouse Harlequin.

Ethnocentric marketing

There is also another reason why global marketing seems less intrusive in the American market. Americans invented in-your-face marketing. And, global marketers speak English. The marketing that anti-globalization adherents are angry about is pretty much the application of American marketing principles in foreign countries, even though, as we have seen, some of the basic assumptions behind those principles are violated. The marketing activities discussed in Chapter 2 are directly from the American playbook, and even the selling orientation criticized at the beginning of this chapter has its clear counterpart in the U.S. market. The reason for this latter fact is that of all the markets in the world, America is probably the most saturated. We need to be sold because we've got everything we need already, as some people claim.

Americans don't feel strange when somebody "toots their own horn." You are on your own, and if nobody else does it, you have to do it yourself. In fact, if you don't make yourself heard, people are going to think that you have nothing to say. It all makes sense, of course, in the low-context/high-mobility culture of the immigrant-friendly U.S. You've got to speak "loud and clear." Virtually all foreign marketers use American advertising agencies for the U.S. market, and some of the most in-your-face ads hype these brands. It's sort of an ultimate homage to American brashness to see a Nissan truck crossing a ditch with two cowboys bouncing on the flatbed.

One might expect the American business schools, where many foreign companies send their best and brightest, to preach a culturally less ethnocentric style of management. But this is not happening. The American business school has become a bastion of American-style business, in marketing, finance, management, and even ethics. There are several reasons for this. One is the general perception that the American model is winning—anyway, that's what the foreigners also come to learn. Another is the American melting-pot tradition, where old customs are replaced by a new low-context amalgam. A third is the traditional academic stress on basic principles, abstractions which supposedly are valid underneath the web of real-world complications such as culture.

To be sure, as the melting-pot tradition has given way in America to multiculturalism, giving each ethnic group and gender its rightful attention, many business schools today are teaching classes aimed to develop cultural sensitivity. This new stress also fits better with the fact that most business today is necessarily international. For the business schools, the problem is that many of the professors have little or no cultural knowledge or sensitivity themselves. This is not because they are all American—there are few places with more diversity than an American business school faculty—but rather that their doctoral training by definition was more in-depth than in the breadth required when tackling cross-cultural issues. They have also been indoctrinated with mantras like "Good marketing is good marketing everywhere," developing a resistance to cultural differences, which also transfers to their peer-reviewed journals.

Thus it is the case that discussions on the marketing of birth-control devices in Bangladesh are led by instructors who have no knowledge of Islam, reminding one of the Japanese teachers of English who cannot speak the language. Encounter groups designed to teach new students from different cultural backgrounds to be sensitive to others are led by professors who ask people to speak about themselves openly in front of strangers, a kind of boot-camp introduction to sensitivity. Placing a premium on verbal communication, teachers force class participation by randomly calling on students, petrifying even the American male "dominators." Students of business ethics are taught how to reason themselves out of ethical dilemmas when underlying values should be sufficient to suggest a solution (perhaps not surprisingly, according to empirical research, students who take courses in business ethics tend to show worse ethical judgment than those without relevant coursework).[3] Understandably, the typical business school graduate emerges with a certain air of insolence, a kind of "damn the torpedoes" attitude reminiscent of that of America's first MBA president.

The Global Threat

In the end, you would expect that people in some countries would find the global brands' marketing efforts to convince them about the worth of a product or service intrusive. If the product and marketing efforts are standardized and based on what is done in other markets, local consumers might feel insulted. In particular, if the global marketer's attitude is ethnocentric and insensitive to local traditions, as Levitt's globalization "imperative" suggests, then anti-globalization reactions could be easily kindled. Given the pre-eminence of American brands and American-style marketing, coupled with a relative lack of cultural sensitivity, you

---

3.   John R. Sparks and Shelby D. Hunt, "Marketing Researcher Ethical Sensitivity: Conceptualization, Measurement, and Exploratory Investigation," *Journal of Marketing,* Vol. 62, April 1998, pp. 92–109.

should not be surprised that anti-globalization sometimes seems very close to anti-Americanism.

Taken together, these factors combine to make global marketing a very potent American threat to many countries and cultures. The reasons are not simply a xenophobic response toward foreign peoples or cultures, or animosity against the biggest and most powerful country in the world presently. The reasons also have to do with the natural instinct of people to preserve what they value, and the natural doubts about the promises of new purveyors whose allegiance may lie elsewhere. And the marketing effort to satisfy these new markets is not quite what we as marketers would ideally like it to be, since global strategies introduce limits on local flexibility. Products and services have a degree of standardization, making them less than perfectly adapted to any given local market. These new products often have definite countries of origin, also challenging the existing order. When these factors come together in an American brand, the effect can be to trigger an individual's more general perception of American power and American culture. The result, depending on the country and the individual, can be the kind of emotional response exemplified in the anti-globalization and anti-American movements.

5 ANTI-GLOBALIZATION AND MARKETING

Back to local?

Anti-globalization headlines in the economic news reached a peak at the beginning of the millennium. But after 9/11, economic anti-globalization demonstrations were overshadowed by more sinister developments. As the headline news after September 11 shifted to a focus on terrorism and the Iraq war, economic globalization issues receded into the background. The anti-globalization movement was more or less transformed into an anti-war force. Demonstrations that once would have attacked the power of the WTO and the spread of American brands instead featured slogans such as "No war for oil" and "No right to kill." Life and death issues trumped economics and marketing.

At a certain level, political and economic issues are not really that distinct. For example, the Americans used economic incentives to try to entice reluctant nations to join the war coalition, and French resistance to the war could be attributed to its economic interests in Iraq. Also, the Iraq attack, ostensibly aimed to eliminate weapons of mass destruction (WMDs), seemed partly designed to safeguard American oil interests, not an unreasonable suspicion given America's continued dependence on oil. Furthermore, as the coalition plans for post-war Iraq were made public, it became clear that the reconstruction efforts would be spearheaded by American multinationals.

American multinationals would harvest what American weap-
ons had sown. Even a pro-globalization person could be for-
given for thinking that America was the real enemy of free
global trade and investment.

Anti-American sentiments have actually been part of the anti-
globalization agenda from the beginning. It was mainly Ameri-
can brands that were being attacked, American multinationals
were among the most aggressive exploiters of low-wage labor,
and the American people were the world's most voracious users
of energy. Successive American administrations had been
among the most ardent supporters of the global free trade insti-
tutions, the World Bank, the IMF, and the WTO. To be anti-glo-
balization and anti-American—and anti-war—was not
contradictory. In the immediate post-war period, the anti-glo-
balization movement seemed less significant and vital than it
had been just a year earlier. It came back, of course, with a ven-
geance at the WTO Cancun meeting.

The Anti-Globalization Case

The anti-globalization movement had gained ground steadily
throughout 2001 before being punctured by the 9/11 events.
Books debating the pros and cons of globalization continued to be
published throughout the rest of the year and into 2002.[1] The
majority of the economic globalization books dealt with the
effects of free trade on jobs and the environment. They detailed
how free trade areas affected local employment in mature economies, the outsourcing by companies and lost jobs for unskilled
labor, and how globalization had shifted the job opportunities
into low-paying service jobs. From the perspective of the low-
wage countries—those that did most of the manufacturing
work—the new jobs were better than nothing. In fact, they were
better than what the local businesses paid, but there was also
plenty of miserable working conditions documented: long hours

---

1.   A search on *Amazon.com* in July 2002 turned up 1,116 titles under
      "globalization."

in sweatshops, the use of child labor, and so on. Environmental degradation was also a big topic and obviously important, but its relationship to marketing activities seemed nonexistent.

There was also a good deal of writing about the often-failing policies of the big international organizations—the World Bank, the IMF, and the WTO—but surprisingly little about the UN. Globalization was seen mainly as an economic phenomenon, tied only indirectly to issues of concern to the UN. Financial integration was a big issue, and the fact that the Multilateral Agreement on Investment had died in 1998 caused some concern. As of 2002, the case for globalizing financial markets, if not product markets, was seriously questioned by a number of observers, not all anti-globalizers.

One striking development was the extent to which the IMF, and to a slightly lesser degree, the World Bank, were denounced. While the institutions had received their share of criticism in the past, it had mainly come from recipients in the third world who suffered under crippling debt and interest payments. It was easy to dismiss that criticism because it was so obviously self-serving, and could be due as much to improper spending and lackluster performance as anything else. Other voices from advanced countries with less obvious biases had been added. A 2002 book by Joseph Stiglitz entitled *Globalization and Its Discontents* was partly a settling of the score with former colleagues at the World Bank and the IMF, but still had a withering attack on the loan conditions imposed by those institutions.[2] Adding salt to the wounds was the recognition that Prime Minister Mahatir's action to stop free capital flow and put in place currency controls in Malaysia in 1998, against IMF advice, turned out to be a very successful move. From Britain came Noreena Hertz's *The Silent Takeover*, arguing that multinational corporations were crushing democracy.[3]

---

2. Joseph E. Stiglitz, *Globalization and Its Discontents* (New York: W.W.Norton), 2002.

3. Noreena Hertz, *The Silent Takeover* (New York: HarperBusiness), 2003.

Newly published World Bank studies were used to question whether in fact the development policies followed for the last decades had produced the growth recorded. Harvard professor Dani Rodrik claimed that the "success" cases of globalization, including South Korea, China, and Japan, scored their advances while protected by import barriers, not the open markets advocated by the IMF advisers.[4] A related argument was made by Alan Rugman, who demonstrated that the increased "global" trade was in fact limited to trade between members of various trade blocs, with only limited trade between blocs. His book bravely pronounced it *The End of Globalization*.[5] Doubts about free trade advantages were also expressed in Tina Rosenberg's *New York Times Magazine* article "The Free-Trade Fix," published August 18, 2002.

Globalization successes?

I was also interested in tracking the effects of globalization on the markets for products and services. A striking fact was that relatively little had been written about the supposedly positive "demand-side" effect. It had clearly been taken for granted, just the way we who teach marketing tend to assume global expansion is welcome. The benefits of free trade were of course a central theme of pro-globalization advocates, but little seemed to have been done to check whether a new and better life had actually been delivered in the marketplace. The reliance on aggregate statistics, such as economic growth and per-capita gross domestic product (GDP), was notable, and the fact that average incomes had indeed risen was taken as evidence that globalization was succeeding according to promise. The scant and unreliable data available on income distribution, an important complementary statistic (after all, I, for one, wanted to know who got the new

---

4. Dani Rodrik, "Free Trade Optimism: Lessons From the Battle in Seattle," *Foreign Affairs*, May–June 2003, p.135.

5. Alan Rugman, *The End of Globalization* (New York: Amacom), 2001. A more upbeat assessment of globalization is offered by Jerry Sullivan, who anticipates that corporations will be forced to be more sensitive to local culture and conditions. Jeremiah J. Sullivan, *The Future of Corporate Globalization* (Westport, CT: Quorum), 2002.

money), suggested that all was not well. While economic growth had been relatively strong in the 1990s, the data on income distribution suggested that inequality might have risen, in the U.S. and Russia in particular, but also in many other countries. Within countries, the rising quality of life was not shared equally, historically a portent for social unrest.

But to find out more about the effects of globalization on the markets for products and services, it was really not necessary to look at the globalization literature. The evidence was all around me. The stores were all selling products and brands from various foreign countries, some of which we had never considered before. There were Kia cars from Korea, Skodas from the Czech Republic, and (although short-lived) Yugos from former Yugoslavia. There was wine from Chile, Australia, and South Africa. Pop groups from Ireland, Sweden, and perhaps less surprisingly, Latin America topped the U.S. charts. Most popular TV cartoons for children came from Japan, which also provided the leading computer games, both reflecting the country's unique obsession with stylized reality, purity, and the fragility of life—bonsai, origami, and geishas of the floating world. Foreign-based retail chains— luxury and apparel brands, of course, but also The Body Shop from the UK (personal care), Carrefour from France and Delhaize from Belgium (food retailing), and IKEA from Sweden (furniture)—succeeded globally where many had failed in the past.

Although not all countries had been inundated to the same degree, there was no doubt that in terms of products and services on the market, economic globalization had succeeded to an astonishing degree. Russians could now buy 2-in-1 shampoos from Unilever, the Chinese invented a novel way to pronounce Coca-Cola (ko-kou-ko-lee) to get the written kanji characters to mean "happiness-in-the-mouth" (after a disastrous phonetic version that came out as "Bite the wax tadpole," whatever that means), and the Nike swoosh logo became a favored symbol of anti-American demonstrators around the world. In terms of products and brands, globalization was coming along very nicely.

But was this a misreading of the evidence? To a large extent, the anti-globalization movement seemed to feed off these very inroads by global brands into foreign markets. The brands were targeted. The attack against McDonald's in France for threatening French farmers' livelihoods, the disparagement of Nike sweatshop practices on the Web, and the ransacking of a KFC restaurant in India for allegedly serving food not permitted under Hindu law were apparently not isolated incidents, but surface manifestations of more deep-seated concerns. Why attack the brands? Why not deal with the concerns directly?

A coalition of the diverse

Who were the anti-globalizers? What exactly did they want? To me, the anti-globalization movement seemed quite confused—and confusing. For example, the justifications for the attacks seemed to vary widely. One group of issues concerned the bad working conditions in the third-world sweatshops, the use of children, and the treatment of women. Another set of issues involved the lack of local commitment on the part of the multinationals, especially with regard to environmental degradation. The power to dominate domestic competitors was also an issue with anti-globalizers, especially as it affected local jobs, traditions, and culture. Adding to the complexity, the anti-globalizers themselves were very varied in their backgrounds. They included high-school kids and 1960s radicals. I found labor unions joining forces with college graduates. There were members of feminist movements, environmental groups, and well-positioned professionals. One of the more active groups, European-based Attac, counted among its members some of the leading intellectuals in Europe.[6] Non-governmental organizations (NGOs) from advanced and developing countries participated, as in the World Social Forum in Brazil in 2002. It seemed true that the overwhelming majority of the protesters were liberal or left-leaning in political terms, but they were not necessarily against all forms of globalization; in fact, many disavowed the anti-globalization label.

There were also indications that anti-globalization sentiments were not necessarily shared equally among advanced and devel-

---

6. Christiane Grefe, Mathias Greffrath, and Harald Schumann, *Attac: Vad vill globaliseringskritikerna?* (Stockholm: Brutus Östling), 2002.

oping countries. While anti-globalization advocates frequently referred to dismal conditions in poorer countries as justifications for rejecting globalization, politicians and citizens of these countries were largely in favor of globalization, although without the financial straitjackets imposed by the IMF. The poor wanted not only jobs, but also the influx of foreign products implied by globalization. It looked as if the anti-globalization demonstrations were based more on frustrations and concerns among the populations in the advanced countries than on the expressed complaints of the poor.

Why did they attack the brands? The most obvious answer was that the brands were symbols of the companies attacked. I could see that the majority of the brands disparaged all were what marketers call "company brands," with brand names the same as the corporation. The Coca-Cola Corporation also sells Sprite and Minute Maid and dozens of other brands, but the attacks were of course against Coca-Cola—no confusion there. The same was true for Levi's, McDonald's, Starbucks, and Nike. Since the corporations were headquartered far away, their brands were an easier target to reach. In the same fashion, when American congressmen wanted to punish Japanese Toshiba for trading prohibited technology with former Soviet Russia, they smashed a Toshiba radio. Also, the brands represented, in many cases, a major portion of a company's assets, and the derogation of a brand could be expected to inflict major damage on its corporation—as in the Coca-Cola bottling problems in Europe in 2001. The intangibility of a brand made it also a particularly convenient target to disparage in communications media such as the Internet, especially for the well-known global brands that everybody recognized.

Not all anti-globalization efforts were directed at individual companies, of course, but at the "whole capitalist system" and the process of globalization. The global brands got hit nevertheless as symbols of this process and the system. The same transference was at work when brands from a particular country—America in particular—were attacked. The brands now represented their countries, as Levi's does America, Chanel does France, and Toyota does Japan. This deduction fit very well with some of my own research in the area of country of origin, which shows that people frequently use the country that a brand is from to evaluate product quality.

Anti-globalizers, for all their diversity of agendas and motivations and demographic makeup, seemed to target major foreign brands and their products as convenient, recognizable, and locally available symbols of globalization. Local workers upset about job loss, local businesspeople angry about foreign competition, radicals upset about the increasing commercialization of society, high-school students protesting sweatshops and child labor in low-wage countries, women demanding equal educational opportunities for women in third-world countries, and traditionalists upset about the loss of local business control could all converge on the attack against the global brands from foreign countries. They might be charging the wrong enemy, and they might not have a very coherent alternative plan, but there were reasons for doing what they did, however confused and confusing the picture from the outside.

"McDonaldization"

The anti-globalization problems with global brands had already been anticipated by some observers. In 1993, sociologist George Ritzer published his book on *The McDonaldization of Society*, coining a phrase that has become synonymous with the commercialization of societies everywhere.[7] In that book, he documented the rise of McDonald's in the American and global economies, and its effect on culture, lifestyles, and consumption habits. Identifying four basic drivers of McDonald's economic superiority—efficiency, calculability, predictability, and control—he traces their role in McDonald's success, not only at home but also overseas.

The message of the book is really not an anti-globalization thesis. Ritzer sees the four principles behind McDonald's success as applicable in a wide variety of settings—in education, in sports, in television, in politics, in employee relations, and so on. He pre-

---

7.   George Ritzer, *The McDonaldization of Society* (Thousand Oaks, CA: Pine Forge Press), 1993.

dicts that these basic principles will transform not only businesses, but whole economies and societies, also overseas. Even though Ritzer recognizes that local cultures might not welcome McDonaldization, most of his work suggests that the economic benefits of the system are sufficiently attractive for the process to be virtually unstoppable. Most strikingly, he predicts that McDonald's itself might well disappear, but McDonaldization will be taken up and implemented by local entrepreneurs.

It is somewhat ironic to realize that McDonaldization as Ritzer presents it is the result of a globalization process that was initially assumed to be mostly benign. I don't mean simply in terms of bringing good things to other people. An early (1954) and prescient essay by David Potter, an eminent historian, promoted the notion that the real benefits of globalization should involve not simply selling better products to other people, but also teaching them how to produce better products on their own.[8] This "technology transfer," as economists call it, is exactly what McDonaldization involves—a new and better business model. In this sense, Ritzer is really not an anti-globalizer.

"McWorld"

The same cannot be said of Benjamin Barber's *Jihad vs. McWorld*, published in 1995.[9] Although the book is a work by a political scientist who is mainly concerned with the survival of democracy, its attack on free markets focuses on how the global expansion of McDonald's and other American brands has come to dominate local markets and local sovereignty.

The first part of the book deals with the emergence of the new global markets, the McWorld. It is a thoroughly documented presentation of the historical development from a resource-driven international order, to the post-World War II hard goods markets, the emergence of branding and software as key sales arguments,

---

8. David M. Potter, *People of Plenty* (Chicago: University of Chicago Press), 1954.

9. Benjamin R. Barber, *Jihad vs. McWorld* (New York: Ballantine Books), 1995.

and the final shift to a service-based knowledge economy. Although the tone is necessarily critical about the impact of McDonaldization on local politics and cultural traditions, most marketers will find much to agree with. In fact, while specific examples might be new, the general thrust is one with which marketers can readily identify, only that they may take more pride in the developments than Barber does. That Nike is no longer simply a shoe company, but really exports "sports" and a "can-do" spirit is precisely what marketers applaud, while Barber is appalled.

Where the book is at its best and most novel is in juxtaposing this increased commercialism against national and local political and cultural interests. Barber points out, quite correctly, that the products and brands introduced into the new markets, unwittingly or not, challenge not only pocketbooks, but also ways of life—less of an issue in emerging markets, perhaps, but still a threat to local traditions. This is easiest to see in what we call lifestyle products and brands, and where, not incidentally, American global corporations are often involved. Fast-food chains not only compete with local businesses, but also influence how people do lunch—briefer than before and often alone. People drive to work when gasoline prices are low, weakening the public transportation system. A Walkman makes music available everywhere, in the process isolating people from their fellow travelers—and so on. In particular, Barber notes with disapproval that, when coupled with deregulation and privatization, the free trade regime actually leads governments to relinquish authority and redefine previously public goods as private (as in the case of airline security, pollution, hospital care, electricity, etc.). Free markets and private choice are good at growing the economy, but not good at distributing the gains. As economists admit, free markets are not fair.

In the book, Barber sets the tribalism of Jihad against the global village of McWorld. Under the fundamentalism of Jihad, instead of open markets, countries close themselves off; instead of globalization, we get nation-states; instead of becoming cosmopolitan, people stay parochial. In either case, whether McWorld or Jihad,

Barber remains skeptical about the prospects for democracy, citing the lack of government in the one case, and too much dictatorial power in the other. In terms of marketing, these issues are of course somewhat remote, but one can infer that as marketers drive McWorld forward, they also help undermine the rule of democracy. Barber reasons that not all decisions by a society can be subjected to the laws of a free market. Because under pressure, local governments will yield to the demands of the multinational firms, allow deregulation and privatization, and start to exercise their legitimate authority over public choices.

According to Barber, the choices presented by marketers are superficial ("You can choose between sixteen brands of toothpaste, eleven models of pickup truck, seven brands of running shoes") when compared with the public choices of infrastructure or environmental policies that are subordinated to the economic benefits of corporations. By the same token, governments become extensions of corporations when dealing with their foreign counterparts. Barber approvingly quotes Paul Krugman's statement that 'governments have consented to a regime that allows markets to boss them around,' forcing choices on the society which no democratic process has vetted."[10]

What are you to make of this polemic against global marketing? For many marketers, the description and analysis can be viewed as largely correct, but the conclusions might seem too far-reaching. Marketers really have no intention of subverting governments or the democratic process. They have brought these new products and brands to the newly opened markets just as they were expected to do. It is also in the nature of things that marketers would try to do their best to develop the market and gain market share, possibly against other brands—one can hardly be faulted for trying to compete. The shift from product marketing to brand marketing simply reflects the realities of the marketplace. With so many products of equal quality, to differentiate oneself, it is necessary to build a strong brand and protect it. In today's markets, it is one of the few competitive advantages that

10. Barber, p. 241.

can be sustained over the long run. Problem is, of course, marketers don't look at the bigger picture.

No logo

Perhaps the most prominent anti-globalization book is *No Logo*
by Naomi Klein, a journalist with the *Toronto Globe & Mail*.[11]
Published in 2000, the book made explicit for the first time the
strong relationship among globalization, dominant global brands,
and losses of domestic alternatives and local jobs.

In her book, Klein divides global brand analysis into four main
parts: No Space, No Choice, No Jobs, and No Logo. The first part,
No Space, documents how ubiquitous brands have become,
invading not only city streets, but hospitals, museums, and universities, branding every aspect of daily life. There is an underlying sense of despair over the inevitable commercialization, and it
is clear that Klein's own sympathies do not rest with the brand
managers.

In the second part of the book, No Choice, Klein elaborates on
the way in which the large global units tend to dominate local
alternatives, reducing the alternatives available in the marketplace. Klein discusses at length how the emergence of large-category killer retail chains ("Big Box stores," as she calls them) has
squeezed many local retailers out of business, an extension of the
branding complaint voiced in the first part of the book.

In No Jobs, Klein deals with the job losses in developed countries
associated with globalization, and also with the treatment of low-
wage workers—poor, uneducated, often women, and sometimes
children—in the sweatshops, a hot issue in many anti-globalization demonstrations. In the last part, No Logo, same as the title of
the book, the discussion offers advice and recipes for anti-globalization activism, one reason the book has become a "bible" for
anti-globalizers.

Klein's book has met with considerable success in Europe, less in
the U.S. The reviews and comments from pro-globalization economists have been predictably negative. Economists argue that

---

11. Naomi Klein, *No Logo* (London: Flamingo), 2000.

even if the workers in the low-wage countries do not make much money, they do make more than their compatriots working for local companies. Also, the global companies transfer production technology to the poor countries, making it possible to gradually improve worker skills and productivity. As for the effect of the global brands, these brands provide the added value that consumers look for. And without the dynamism that comes with competition, the rate of innovation would be reduced.

In her defense, Klein is concerned with more than just economics. Once the social and human costs of job loss and relocation and the effects on traditional modes of living are added into the equation, globalization can be traumatic. Even if the discomfort is temporary, the length of the transition period is uncertain, and the light at the end of the tunnel is weak and flickering.

Market power

Two of Klein's anti-globalization arguments that relate directly to marketing are worth further elaboration. One concerns *market power*, the threat of dominance by global players over domestic firms and their subsequent demise. The second is the notion that increasing globalization leads to more homogeneity among markets and countries. Both arguments derive from the economic benefits of large scale.

The basic argument is quite simple: Large global units tend to dominate local alternatives, reducing the options available in the marketplace and the job opportunities. Part of this process revolves around the strength of global brands, but reaches further into the business of franchising, consolidation, and company mergers and acquisitions. As a typical example, anti-globalizers refer to the emergence of large-category killer retail chains that have squeezed many local retailers out of business. The arrival of a new Wal-Mart store outside a small town allegedly forces local stores to close and reduces the downtown's value as a shopping destination, gradually transforming it into a ghost town. The new jobs created at Wal-Mart to replace eliminated jobs are at minimum-wage levels, and while local suppliers in non-competing lines of businesses relocate around the new Wal-Mart Big Box, they are still threatened by the possibility of Wal-Mart extending into their lines.

As Wal-Mart expands overseas, there is little reason why foreign countries should welcome its entry. Rather, as has happened in several small communities in the U.S., a better policy might be for the local municipalities to actively discourage entry, and certainly not encourage it with tax abatement and other incentives. It is striking to realize that the Wal-Mart example is also used as one principal illustration of the need for global dominance in the corporate strategy advice offered by management consultants. The same aspects that infuriate anti-globalizers are used as motivators for a corporate globalization imperative.[12]

The successful operation of these chains depends on economies of scale that allow low cost and low prices. To exploit these advantages to the fullest requires expansion into new markets. This is accomplished using a clustering approach that some writers liken to scorched earth policy. For example, Starbucks, the chain of cafes serving a wide menu of different coffees, attempts to blanket new urban markets with a large number of stores in close proximity, allowing customers to find a Starbucks within walking distance in any city. The resulting dominance has a homogenizing effect that is exacerbated by the requirement to avoid local variations to minimize costs. Anti-globalizers are especially scornful of the "censorship" they detect in the enforcement of standardized dress, language, sexual mores, and clerk behavior. The servers in McDonald's are asked to dress the same, use the same greeting, and smile the same way, thus impersonalizing personal service.

Anti-globalizers also make a direct link between global dominance and outsourcing manufacturing jobs. The relocation of manufacturing to low-wage countries is of course a staple of pro-globalization—and anti-globalization—arguments. That is, with the reduced tariffs that come with open access to markets, importing from a low-wage country is made feasible. Most companies, trying to be more cost-efficient and competitive, recognize the advantages to produce in the lowest wage country that can

---

12. Vijay Govindarajan and Anil K. Gupta, *The Quest for Global Dominance* (San Francisco: Jossey-Bass), 2001.

still be counted on to provide infrastructure and a docile labor force. It is the treatment of the workers—poor, uneducated, often women, and sometimes children—in the sweatshops that has been an issue in many anti-globalization demonstrations. When the multinationals cut costs, they do it on the backs of the poor.

Same everywhere?

A second major complaint against globalization is that local alternatives, local brands, local color, and local culture are all lost. The notion is that the massive marketing effort supporting the global brand cannot be matched by the local business, which has to sell out (often to the global entry) and withdraw from the market. Empirically, this argument would seem to have much validity in that one can see global brands capturing a large share of many markets while local brands falter. Examples range from the incursion of Japanese cars into Western markets to the unlikely success of Corona beer in old Europe.

The loss of local favorites is clearly a matter of great concern to activists, especially where the elimination of local choices might be due to aggressive price-cutting by new entrants. Of course, it is not clear whether the quality of the local products is competitive or whether the successes really are a matter of massive promotion and price cuts alone. In other cases, the new entrants are likely to increase the total market size by offering functionality not available before. The local resistance against the IKEA furniture chain around the world has been abated as competitors realize the benefits of having young couples and single people come into the market.

According to this argument, as local brands falter, the invasion by global brands has meant that the marketplaces around the world have become more homogeneous, losing their local idiosyncrasies. This complaint figures not only in terms of extinct differences between countries and cultures, but also in terms of products and services. Automobiles using state-of-the-art technology and new design features turn out to be almost indistinguishable. The various brands of running shoes all perform equally well. Symphony orchestras that once had unique and recognizable instrumental characteristics and approaches to the musical masterworks now sound the same as the musicians are all schooled in the same way, the instruments are the best in the world, and they are all led by the same globetrotting conductors.

Local Resurgence

As many observers have pointed out, the marketplaces around the world might have grown more homogeneous in some ways, but they have also come to display much more variety than previously. Although one may find the same global brands everywhere—the logos for Coca-Cola, Sony, and Volkswagen are as ubiquitous as Naomi Klein claims—it is also true that the variety in each local market has increased considerably, especially those most open to globalization. As cultural sociologists have documented, the impact of globalization in many countries has been to stimulate a new interest in traditional culture. Whether this interest is due to the anti-globalization movement or not is open to question, but the demonstrations have certainly helped stimulate local initiatives.

Of course, there is little doubt that globalization has meant that consumer culture for the young has changed toward the world model. The brand names discussed throughout this book have become the norm for teenagers in countries as different as China, Turkey, South Africa, and Hungary. As borders open up, American jeans, fast food, and leisurewear—and, of course, films, MTV, and TV programs—have become emblematic of the new freedom—so have Sony's Walkman and Nintendo's Game Boy from Japan. There is also consistency in the way these icons of the world's popular culture are enjoyed, as much for the social status they confer as for their intrinsic benefits.

But digging deeper, there are differences. In China, the proximity to Hong Kong, Taiwan, and other Asian countries with Chinese minorities has made for a strong presence of Chinese pop songs, martial-arts films, and soap operas. In Turkey, there is a resurgence of Islamic traditions in fashion, music, and art, complementing the new influences and creating a decidedly Oriental version of consumerism. In South Africa, the history of English and Dutch colonial presence has meant that European influences are still strong in fashion, foods, and clothing, but the African indigenous culture is also resurgent, and is likely to become gradually stronger. In Hungary, the new influences co-exist with the old Austro-Hungarian cabaret culture, with Magyar music, and with traces of communist traditions in media control.[13]

The new local advantage

Over time, open markets and globalization have inspired domestic entrepreneurs and initiatives. The standardization and economies of scale of global brands are still there, but local firms are capitalizing on the anti-global sentiments of consumers. This is happening not only among the patriotic segments and anti-American countries of the world, but more generally. In addition, market growth can lead to a situation where local companies can reach economies of scale and efficient size within the domestic market. The large fixed plant costs that underlie the need for product standardization can be recouped quicker with a larger home market. Flexible manufacturing systems make it possible to gain cost efficiencies without producing one single-model version. Localization forces are challenging the global brands.

In May 2003, I participated in a colloquium celebrating the 20th anniversary of Ted Levitt's "The Globalization of Markets" at the Harvard Business School.[14] A select group of academicians and executives gathered to debate to what extent the Levitt advice had proven correct and whether it was still valid. With some surprise, the participants discovered a general consensus that originally the advice had some validity and success, but the pendulum was now swinging back from globalization toward localization.

---

13. These examples come from Peter L. Berger and Samuel P. Huntington, eds., *Many Globalizations* (New York: Oxford University Press), 2003.
14. "The Globalization of Markets: A Colloquium in Appreciation of the Scholarship of Professor Theodore Levitt," *Harvard Business School*, May 28–30, 2003.

The tone was set at the outset by Sir Martin Sorrell, the chief executive of WPP, one of the largest advertising agency groups in the world, and an early proponent of the Levitt thesis. Sir Martin, later echoed by other participants, claimed that although initial globalized efforts had been successful, increased affluence in many markets had made local consumers demand more variety and less standardization. With the exception of the business-to-business markets, where globalization and standardization still dominated, the consensus was that companies now needed to customize their offerings to local preferences. While productivity gains through standardization and globalization were still to be realized in the supply chains, when it came to the demand side and market presence, localization was the new imperative.

Apart from increasing wealth, the conference participants explored other factors in favor of localization. One was that as markets grew, purely local firms could also gain economies of scale. In fact, in an analysis of Rupert Murdoch's 1995 acquisition of the STAR television network in Asia, justified on the basis of cost efficiencies in utilizing Western programming, Pankaj Ghemawat showed how national stations with local programming soon emerged under the STAR umbrella, capturing large shares of the national markets and forcing STAR to localize its own programming. In a similar twist of the received wisdom from Levitt, to remain competitive, global firms have at times had to localize by acquiring strong local businesses and keeping the local brand names intact. Nestle, the Swiss multinational in food and related products, has had a long history of such a strategy, but now McDonald's (buying up Chipotle, the Tex-Mex chain) and others are following suit. MTV, the music television station that started its overseas expansion featuring American artists—on the premise that American music and entertainment were what the rest of the teenage world wanted—has re-oriented its programming to feature more local music and musicians.

The new cola war
This return to local roots is also expressed in the introduction of local brands challenging the dominance of global entries. A good example is the emergence of alternative cola brands to challenge

the dominant American brands, Coca-Cola and Pepsi. As the war in Iraq drew near, Muslims and other antiwar groups found it increasingly unacceptable to purchase American brands, but to quench their thirst for a refreshing cola, they had little choice until Mecca Cola and other colas came along.

There is today, improbably, a new "cola war." The term "cola war" used to refer to the competitive battle between Coca-Cola and Pepsi, stimulated by the blind test results favoring perennial underdog Pepsi. It has lately come to refer to the array of new colas introduced to challenge the Americans, especially—but not exclusively—in Muslim countries.

The most prominent new entry is Mecca Cola, named after the Islamic holy city. The cola is the brainchild of Tawfik Mathlouti who runs a radio station for France's Muslim minority. As the conflict between the U.S. and Iraq unfolded, Mathlouthi was distressed to see his children imbibing their usual Coca-Colas and decided to do something about it.[15] He worked closely with French chemists to develop a formula very similar to Coke's, but less sugary, and spent months organizing an efficient bottling and distribution network. In November 2002, Mecca Cola was launched. The cola proved a hit with Muslim customers first in France and in other countries as well, including the Middle East. By early December, more than one million bottles had been delivered. The standard 1.5-liter bottles carry labels whose bright red and sweeping white script are intentionally reminiscent of Coca-Cola.[16] The cola can be found in Britain, Belgium, and Germany, and bids from companies wanting to become local distributors are pouring in from around the world. Mecca Cola carries the slogan "No more drinking stupid, drink with commitment," and gives 20% of its profits to charity, including Palestinian humanitarian aid.

---

15. John Tagliabue, "They Choke on Coke, but Savor Mecca Cola," *The New York Times,* December 31, 2002, p. 4.
16. N. Janardhan, "Middle East: Watch Out Coke, Here Comes Mecca Cola," *Inter Press Service*, January 23, 2003.

The success of Mecca Cola has sparked local sales of existing alternative colas as well. In the United Arab Emirates, a regional version called Star Cola has seen sales explode. Iran's own Zam Zam Cola, which replaced Pepsi when Ayatollah Khomeini drove out American businesses, has difficulty satisfying demand for its drink.[17] It exports to neighboring Muslim countries and has now been launched in Europe, targeting the Muslim diaspora. New imitations have also cropped up. In March 2003, two new colas, Muslim Up and Arab Cola, were launched in France. Although meant to appeal to young Arabs and support Muslim causes, the brands also try to cash in on the general anti-American sentiment.

The new cola war has had some effects on the American brands' bottom lines. Pepsi's foreign sales were flat during the last part of 2002 and early 2003. Coca-Cola has lost about 10% of sales in the Middle East, and the consumer boycott of American brands has hit its businesses in Bahrain, Lebanon, and Saudi Arabia. The company is reportedly considering a legal challenge against Mecca Cola's packaging and logo, claiming copyright infringement. In the end, unless the new colas start appealing to a large share of the total market, some experts remain quite sanguine. Jagdish Sheth, a marketing professor at the Goizueta Business School at Emory University in Atlanta, argues that the new colas will remain niche products, not really cutting into Coke's main business outside of Muslim markets. The Goizueta School, coincidentally, is named after Roberto Goizueta, the late CEO of Coca-Cola.[18]

Global localization

In response to the increased interest in local traditions, global brands today avoid following a standardized formula for their

---

17. Nassim Majidi and Christina Passarielo, "After Iraq, Cola Wars Heat Up; Muslim Alternatives to Coke and Pepsi Are Springing Up All Across Europe. How Far Can Religious Solidarity Go as a Marketing Strategy?" *Business Week Online*, April 17, 2003.

18. Jagdish Sheth appeared on CNNFN with David Haffenreffer, *War in Iraq*, March 27, 3002.

offerings in different markets. While the early globalization thrust pretty much followed a recipe of increased standardization of products to capture scale and scope economies, as the GDP per capita has grown, so has the demand for increased localization. In this there are distinct differences between developed and less-developed countries. The adaptations required for poorly developed markets tend to be less in terms of product formulation to customer preferences and more in terms of customizing to specific usage conditions. This typically means smaller packages because of less storage capacity and lower per-purchase outlays (as for razor blades by Gillette in third-world countries), simple construction and easy repairs (as for bicycles made for China), robust functionality under severe conditions (Bajaj auto in India, for example), and so on. For these kinds of markets, large in terms of population but with limited average purchasing power, small *is* beautiful.

In more developed markets, the local demands typically revolve around preferences for specific features and adapted formulations that better fit the preferences of the local target segments. A good example of such localization is the way McDonald's has been able to succeed in the French market despite the anti-globalization attacks and any anti-American sentiment there. McDonald's France spent lavishly to refit restaurants with chic interiors and music videos, creating an atmosphere that induced visitors to linger over a meal, contrary to the efficiency-oriented McDonald's in the states. Instead of streamlining menus, items such as hot ham-and-cheese sandwiches dubbed Croque McDo were added, further establishing McDonald's as a destination restaurant. After the Jose Bove-led attack on a McDonald's in the south of France in 1999, the company took out newspaper ads showing fat, ignorant Americans who could not understand why McDonald's used locally produced food that wasn't genetically modified. The self-deprecating effort worked. Because of the success, those at McDonald's headquarters in Illinois have looked the other way in the face of such irreverence and deviations from the standard formula. McDonald's France was reprimanded, however, in early 2003 when the chain took out ads saying that it was not necessarily good to eat at McDonald's every day of the week.[19] "Enough is enough," as headquarters in Illinois demanded the ads be pulled.

A Wake-up Call

In the end, the anti-globalizers might not have won the war exactly, but they have achieved a number of things. Gone is the optimism of globalization at the end of the millennium, and even though the reasons might have more to do with the war on terrorism, the dot-com demise, the SARS threat, and similar external events, the anti-globalization movement can take some credit (or blame, depending on your viewpoint). This can be seen when the pro-globalization books from a couple of years ago are re-read in the new context. For example, a best-selling book such as Thomas Friedman's *Lexus and the Olive Tree*, published in 1999, is relentless in pushing the global imperative.[20] Coining phrases such as "The Golden Straitjacket" and the "Electronic Herd," the book exhorts countries to play by the rules of the free market (the Straitjacket) and the extra-national power of international finance (the Herd) lest they fall behind the countries that do. The anti-globalization movement has helped make such exhortations seem exaggerated and naive. As anti-globalization sentiments have been further kindled by political and military conflict, localization has become the new imperative.

On the other hand, at the level of individual enterprise, the pro-globalization books' more or less implicit message remains very valid: Open and free markets will stimulate not only entry by global companies, but also initiatives by local entrepreneurs. The shift from globalization to localization in company strategies reflects this powerful influence on local entrepreneurship. But, it is not always sufficient for budding entrepreneurs to spot

---

19. Marian Burros, "McDonald's France Says Slow Down on the Fast Food," *The New York Times*, October 30, 2002, p. C1.

20. Thomas L. Friedman, *The Lexus and the Olive Tree*, (New York: Farrar Straus Giroux), 1999.

a possible demand niche emerging in the market for a local variant as the market grows. There also has to be a supportive entrepreneurial environment, a modicum of education in how to run a business, and access to investment capital. These are all things that the globalization process was supposed to bring, but has not always delivered.

6 WHY ONLY AMERICAN BRANDS?

The price of youth

When analyzing anti-globalization protests, it is easy to get the impression that the attacks on brands consistently target only American brands. This is very much in line with the more popular writings on globalization. For example, Thomas L. Friedman suggests that globalization "...wears Mickey Mouse ears, it eats Big Macs, it drinks Coke..."[1] Books critical of marketing's role in globalization such as The McDonaldization of Society and Jihad vs. McWorld use American icons to symbolize what's wrong with the new commercialized society.

The anti-globalizers disparage the brands for their bad practices, with third-world sweatshops, environmental degradation, and ruthless market dominance. Knowing something about the multinationals from other countries, it is hard to believe that these bad practices are limited only to American brands. And in fact, non-American brands are attacked as well. A simple test is to check the index of Naomi Klein's No Logo book.[2] Her book, published in 2000, has the advantage of pre-dating the war on terrorism and Iraq, which turned the anti-globalizers into anti-war demonstrators. Klein mentions—more or less disparagingly—approximately 150 brands, a pretty large number when

---

1. Friedman, p. 309.
2. Klein, op.cit., 2000.

you think of it. Of these, 120, or 80%, are American, a clear majority. Still, some well-known non-American brands are criticized as well—Shell oil for its Nigerian activities, adidas for closing its German plants, and The Body Shop for appropriating women's issues, among others.

To get a better fix on whether American brands are unfairly singled out, we can compare the 80% to the percentage of American brands among global brands in general. In most listings of global brands, American brands are in the majority. Because of that, you might expect more American brands to be disparaged, regardless. Checking this, I found that among Interbrand's Top 100 list for 2002, exactly two-thirds (67%) were American. Comparing this number to the percentage of American brands listed in Klein's index, there is some evidence that American brands are attacked more frequently. Of course, this does not necessarily mean they are "unfairly" singled out; they may in fact be the worst offenders.

This chapter focuses on the question of whether and why American brands are particularly "at risk." Are these brands really worse than others, or is it simply anti-Americanism at work?

The American Problem

I don't want to be too academic, but to get at this question, we need to distinguish between two quite separate forces. On the one hand, the motivation could be *intrinsic*, meaning that the brands are simply attacked for being bad products or doing bad things to their suppliers, the environment, or for some other reason. The fact that they are American brands is not significant. This is possible, and undoubtedly there is some truth to it, but given the percentages in Klein's book, I thought it unlikely to be the whole story. On the other hand, American brands may be attacked because they represent America. We can call this *extrinsic* motivation. That is, the brands are not attacked for what their image is, or what corporation they represent, but for what country they represent. America, after all, represents globalization to many people, as Friedman asserted—and America is the big bully.

Let's examine *intrinsic* motivation further. There are actually a couple of reasons why it is more than a coincidence that American brands are the only ones hit. One is that the American brands are particularly bad—Wal-Mart is worse than French Carrefour, Nike is worse that German Puma, McDonald's is worse than Japanese Mosburger. But this is not a very convincing case. Because of McDonaldization, the business models don't differ that much between the competitors in one industry. A more likely reason might be that the targeted brands are the biggest in their industry. As we have seen, anti-globalizers tend to attack the biggest brands, partly because of their newsworthiness and lack of underdog sympathy—more "bang for the buck." Naomi Klein explains the choice of McDonald's by quoting the McSpotlight Web site: "Due to its massive public prominence and indisputable arrogance...a symbol of all corporations pursuing their profits at any price."[3] There is a presumption that smaller brands will change with the big brands; when Nike stops using child labor, so will the other shoe companies. So, judging from their words and actions, the anti-globalizers consciously target bigger brands. But, are all the biggest brands American brands? This is hardly the case. But the fact is that American brands are the leaders in the product categories most likely to be disparaged, and this might be a clue to what is going on.

Few products targeted

One striking aspect of anti-globalization is that the branding attacks focus on so few product categories. For example, the brands discussed at some length in *No Logo* include athletic shoes (Nike, Reebok, and adidas), fast food (McDonald's, Starbucks), soft drinks (Coca-Cola, Pepsico), retailers (Wal-Mart, The Body Shop, Blockbuster, Borders), entertainment and toys (Disney, MTV, Barbie), and teenage apparel (Calvin Klein, Gap, Levi's, Diesel, Tommy Hilfiger). Automobiles are barely mentioned; neither are consumer electronics (except Microsoft, with a discussion that focuses on the company's labor practices). In fact, consumer durables are basically absent, and so are the supermar-

---

3.   Klein, p. 422.

ket staples of frequently purchased products, from shampoo and detergent to paper products to food and drink.

What could be the explanation for this imbalance? Are the companies in these other product categories blameless? Possibly, but that is hard to believe. Perhaps they do not exploit the benefits of globalization. However, there is evidence that they surely do. Automobiles, computers, and electronics are some of the most globalized of industries. Don't they advertise? They do, and a lot. According to *Advertising Age* estimates, worldwide advertising spending in 2001 stood at $19.3 billion for automobiles, $11.2 billion for food, $10.3 billion for personal care products, $6.6 billion for electronics and computers, and $6.3 billion for media and entertainment.[4]

Several likely scenarios could explain the narrow focus on a few product categories. The first one is simply that working conditions are better, environmental degradation is of no concern, and market efforts are more muted. Given that at least the electronics-based industries tend to present themselves as "clean" industries, environmental effects in those industries should not be a problem. But the working conditions are not so obviously superior: The women in the electronics plants are worked hard, for example, and even in a country like Japan, female workers are housed in dormitories with limited social hours, threatened with dismissal if they get pregnant or married. As for market domination, the competitive battle is as fierce as in any industry, if not more so, and in-your-face advertising is certainly not an unknown in automobile ads.

Cheap and convenient

A better explanation is that the disparaged product categories are those where products are differentiated more through price and promotion rather than functional product differences. This is likely to be the case either where products are standardized (making price important) or where image matters (making pro-

---

4. "Global Marketers," *Advertising Age Special Report*, November 11, 2002, p. 28.

motion important). Both McDonald's and Wal-Mart compete on price, while the other brands in the list compete mainly on advertising and other promotional tactics. Wal-Mart's customers like the everyday low prices and McDonald's attractiveness has a lot to do with the low prices. As for promotional-based strategies, functional differences do perhaps exist among Reebok, adidas, and Nike, but the major selling tool really is the image of the brand.

There is another factor that enhances this effect. These product categories are likely to be in a mature market stage in most advanced countries (although probably not in third-world countries). This means that many potential customers would already have established preferences and loyalties to existing brands, typically local brands. Any new global entries would have to succeed by taking market share away from existing brands, possibly eliminating some favored alternative (as we saw in earlier chapters). These global brands, with their greater resources, lower prices, and increased promotion, end up dominating the locals, the process denounced by anti-globalizers. This process would also help explain why consumer durables in general might have aroused less animosity. The new automobiles, the new electronics gear, and the new mobile phones seem more justified, offering new features, improved functionality, and even creating new markets.

There is also the fact that these product categories carry strong American lifestyle associations. That is, eating at McDonald's and shopping at Wal-Mart are all part and parcel of the American lifestyle. It might seem farfetched, but many, if not all, of these brands really do conjure up a certain picture of an American way of life. It is clearly not an indigenous European or Asian or Latin-American culture, but the convenience-oriented and youth-centered American ethos, especially since many of the products are not adapted to local markets. If this culture-bound explanation has some validity, it would help to explain why it is the American brands that are being disparaged. It reflects a common theme among foreign observers: "These kinds of products Americanize our society and that's what we don't like."

Thus, the evidence suggests that if alleged misdeeds occur on the supply side—third-world sourcing, environmental degradation, and so on—anti-globalization protests might emerge regardless of what country, what product category, or what brands are involved. On the other hand, when it comes to the demand side and what happens to the brands in the marketplace, the anti-globalizers' focus is narrower. The brands in the "high-risk" zone are the brands that try to defeat incumbent locals with standardized products, lower price, and more promotion, in product categories where markets are mature and competition for share is intense, and where there are strong non-traditional lifestyle implications toward the American way of life. These are lesser problems in many third-world countries, which seem to welcome the global influence, and among young people, who seem to welcome the American influence.

The Japanese Case

Why aren't Japanese brands disparaged? Out of the 150 brands mentioned by Naomi Klein, only 3 are Japanese: Sony, Suzuki, the motorcycle manufacturer, and Daishowa-Marubeni, a paper and pulp company. The Suzuki example involves the company's dealings with the Burmese military junta governing the country, and reports on a rock band refusing to perform under Suzuki banners in a company-sponsored concert. Daishowa-Marubeni's problems with logging in Canada's Alberta province on land claimed by the Cree Indians are used by Klein to show how attacking a company's customers—in this case, pizza restaurants and clothing retailers—can force a relatively anonymous company to back down. The Sony discussion revolves around the 1998 *Godzilla* movie fiasco and is of more significance here since it deals with a marketing failure. The film flopped despite a carefully orchestrated launch, an IMC strategy that included a Madison Square Garden premiere, a year-long "teaser campaign" that alone cost $60 million, and an initial coverage of about 20% of all U.S. screens. The failure, according to Klein, was due to the negative word of mouth generated by the opening night audience. In one way, the fiasco was another win for the anti-marketers, but in a more positive vein, it was also a sign that all the marketing in the world won't help an inferior product.

By and large, Japanese brands are not disparaged much. Perhaps it is the relative distance, Japan really being far away from both Europe and the U.S. But, Japanese corporations certainly have prominent global brands. A short list would include some of the top power brands in the world as ranked by British Interbrand, a brand consulting company, or by Young & Rubicam, an American ad agency. And they have strong global presence: Panasonic, Sony, Sharp, and Toshiba in consumer electronics; Honda, Toyota, and Nissan in cars; Yamaha, Kawasaki, Suzuki, and Honda in motorcycles; Nintendo and Sega in toys; Canon, Minolta, Nikon, Olympus, and Pentax in cameras; Seiko and Citizen in watches; Kanebo and Shiseido in cosmetics, and so on. Just listing the brands and product categories gives a clue to the answer as to why they have not been attacked. The products where the Japanese excel are largely consumer durables, not the convenient and frequently purchased products where the Americans have made their mark. These are products where features matter and where technology is likely to dominate habits and cultural traditions. As my Japanese colleagues like to say, "Japanese companies make products with a dream."

This is surely not the whole explanation. You need only think of the American congressmen smashing a portable Toshiba radio to protest the company's Soviet sales. The fact that the product was a consumer durable in fact facilitated the demonstration and made it more relevant when compared to trashing a McDonald's restaurant (which, after all, is typically run by a native compatriot). It is true that technology-based products tend to cross cultural barriers more easily. Most people want the same things from a camera, a television set, or a CD player. Technology also creates new markets, as in video cameras, DVDs, and mobile phones. Even though the Japanese are not necessarily the inventors, their products tend to embody the newest technology, and they open up new possibilities— "Do you dream Sony?" as the ads suggest.

There are actually several reasons why one might have anticipated anti-globalization protests to include more Japanese
brands. The Japanese have surely been beneficiaries of the open
and free markets associated with globalization. They also had the
advantage for many years after World War II to protect their own
home market from foreign imports, allowing their domestic companies a protracted—and protected—gestation period. The Japanese performance in World War II surely did not make many
friends abroad, especially among Koreans and Chinese. If the
motivation behind the attacks is nationalism, you would surely
expect Japan to get its (more than) fair share of disparagement.

Japanese uniqueness

The fact is, of course, that Japan does not closely match the U.S.
in bullying quotient. The size of the country and its lack of military prowess are only a small part of the reason. Another reason
might be that the Japanese do not approach foreign markets with
the assumption that their values are universal and with the confidence in their own system that Americans possess. Their
approach is quite the contrary. The Japanese do not believe that
their values are universal, and they have no confidence that their
way can be a model for others. When they feel superior, as before
World War II, they become merely arrogant, not missionary as
the Americans do. Americans might seem arrogant to many people, but this comes mainly from the blithe assumption that others
will recognize that the American way is the best for all. Americans are reluctant imperialists.

In a sense, paradoxically, this difference makes local adaptation
natural for the Japanese and unnatural for the Americans. "This
succeeded in Japan, therefore it will succeed elsewhere," is not
something any Japanese company would adhere to, yet Americans do it often. It affects not only product design, although that
is the most obvious instance, but the rest of the marketing program, including advertising, distribution, service, and so on. It
does not extend to the upstream supply chain. The Japanese corporation has always been very reliant on a network of semi-
independent supplier firms, and these firms often move with the
company to foreign countries. They also maintain centralized

decision-making in Tokyo at the top management level. Although things are changing, because of the need to closely share technology and control quality, Japanese corporations have had trouble outsourcing to foreign suppliers. This has protected them from the accusations of exploiting low-wage labor in the third world leveled against Western firms.

On the marketing side, the Japanese have relied on local non-Japanese. The advertising done by Japanese companies in the U.S. is done by American ad agencies, in Europe by Europeans. Pricing and positioning are done by local subsidiaries, usually run by native managers—although joined by Japanese expatriate observers from headquarters. The distribution networks employed necessarily involve natives, but with few exceptions the Japanese have always been careful to deal with the middle layer in ways that fit the local culture. The exceptions are all the more noteworthy because they are so few, typically involving questions about sexual discrimination and feudal-style top-down managerial attitudes among some traditional hardliners. In a sense, the great differences between the corporate world in Japan and elsewhere has helped the accommodation: The Japanese way is so obviously unworkable in the more democratic West. As many observers of Japanese business practices point out, a successful manager in Japan is probably the last person the company should send to a Western subsidiary. The top-down hierarchical style of a traditional Japanese manager does not go over well in more egalitarian environments.

The typical Japanese way of adapting a product's design to a foreign market is to first observe the usage conditions and typical behavior of the potential customers in that market. Next, the leading brands in the market are examined and disassembled in an effort to find their strengths and weaknesses, and to pinpoint required features and measurements. This all sounds simple and straightforward, but it requires sensitivity and an eye for detail— Japanese strengths. For example, observing the way a woman driver enters a car showed Honda Prelude designers the need to lower the door threshold and move the emergency break to the middle. To design the lift-back Civic, an observation post in the parking lot of Disneyland in Los Angeles tracked the typical height needed for the door to swing up, and the fact that young children were the ones usually asked to open the door. Toyota's invention of the car coffee-holder is legendary, coming after observing all the drivers of big American cars balancing their coffee cups while navigating the traffic jams in Los Angeles. Once noted, all of us can see these things. But, if you are taught to ignore differences and stick to your own way, these nuances generally go unnoticed.

Japanese quality

Prodded by the Japanese, Western competitors have now learned these practices. Taking apart competing products—reverse-engineering—has now become standard procedure among most competitors in consumer durables. It's part of the benchmarking drive, figuring out what makes competitors strong—and weak. The first customer for any new model on the market is typically the competition, unless a prototype was leaked before the release. The classic case is, again, Toyota's use of the Volkswagen Beetle to redesign and improve its own Toyopet model and then the Corolla when going abroad. It was used again for the development of the Lexus, using several disassembled Mercedes models. Reverse-engineering requires not only engineering expertise and patience, but also an attitude that rejects the "not invented here" syndrome. You cannot be defensive when doing this; it's like asking yourself, "What did they do right and where did we go wrong?" This is not easy in individualistic cultures, but again, it is well-suited to the Japanese style of teamwork.

In a sense, even though product categories do not reflect culture per se, the Japanese character shines through in its care to adapt to local conditions. Their advertising in America is as American as anyone's, that is, it is as in your face as you can get. Channels of distribution are run by Americans. Their marketing programs in other countries follow pretty much the same patterns, adapted to the local conditions. Their products are also adapted to local conditions. But in the supply chain and channels of distribution, this adaptation has also involved upgrading many of the middle layer's operations, especially in delivering superior customer service. Thus, the adaptation was done without sacrificing the workmanship, customer service, and quality of the Japanese home market. That is, while the Japanese have adapted to the customers' usage conditions and preferences, they have also provided superior products and services. It is no overstatement to say that the inroads of Japanese companies in the world's markets have raised the standards of these markets to new performance levels.

It is this phenomenon, more than anything else, that makes the Japanese brands unlikely targets of anti-globalization forces. The contrast with American inroads and dominance is striking. The successful products and services from the Americans involve, as we have seen, increased convenience, less expense, and youth-oriented offerings sold mainly through low price and promotion. Small wonder if the world feels "McDonaldized"; these brands often represent a lowest common denominator of consumption, the emblematic waste which, according to *Affluenza*, makes even Americans sick.

These differences between Japanese and American products are reflected also in each country's approach to quality. For some years in the 1980s and 1990s, it was thought that American products would never be up to Japanese standards. The vaunted Japanese techniques of "quality circles" never seemed to work in American companies. To help close the gap, the American Quality Foundation enlisted the help of G. Clotaire Rapaille, a French cultural anthropologist. Using in-depth interviews with workers, Rapaille discovered that the very meaning of "quality" seemed to differ between the two cultures. While in Japan quality meant zero defects (i.e., perfection), the Americans' sense of quality was a pragmatic "It works."[5] Once the differences were clarified, successful adjustments could be made in the way quality circles were implemented in the U.S.—the goal of zero defects was rescinded.

---

5. G. Clotaire Rapaille, *7 Secrets of Marketing* (Provo, Utah: Executive Excellence Publishing), 2001, p. 241.

The European Case

If Japanese products represent a Zen-like effort to attain perfection while American products stress imperfect but life-affirming hedonism, what can one say about the global brands out of Europe? More importantly, to what extent have the anti-globalizers attacked European brands, or have they?

First a caveat: Despite the rhetoric in the European Union (EU) and elsewhere, it is probably premature to talk of a homogeneous "European" culture that could animate the products offered. In the quality example above, Rapaille found that in Germany, quality meant "standards," and in France, quality meant "luxury."[6] These definitions were obviously not very similar. On the other hand, with Europeans frequently grouped together in discussing anti-globalization as well as anti-Americanism, it seems necessary to explore if "European" brands are disparaged as often as American brands.

Of the 29 non-U.S. brands (out of a total of 150 brands) indexed in *No Logo*, 19 are European. So, European brands are also disparaged, even though the percentage (13%) is not high.[7] The European brands criticized at some length number only five: Absolut Vodka from Sweden, adidas and Bertelsmann from Germany, Benetton from Italy, and The Body Shop from England. Note the relative absence of French brands, particularly the globally well-known luxury brands. Only Yves Saint Laurent and Christian Lacroix are even mentioned, and very briefly at that. Of course, the imbalance might well be a reflection of the North American perspective of the book, but again, one is struck by the product categories disparaged; they are very similar to those attacked among the American brands.

What do the European brands get disparaged for? The Absolut Vodka and Benetton brands exemplify the way brand-building

---

6.   Ibid, p. 244.

7.   As before, to make the comparison properly, one ought to account for the total number of brands from the various geographical regions involved. In the 2002 *Interbrand* listing of the top 100, 25% were European brands compared to 67% American and 5% Japanese.

advertising incorporates and exploits cultural movements to create affinity with their target segments. This attribute is not very objectionable to true marketers; in fact, it is quite according to script. Bertelsmann, the German publishing company, and Britain's (or, more accurately, Anita Roddick's) The Body Shop, the personal care products store chain, are seen as examples of the "octopus-like" expansion of global companies across countries, and the clone-like store environment of The Body Shop is seen as an example of the homogenizing force of globalization. The Body Shop disparagement is in a sense surprising, since the chain is guided very much by an ethos of environmental concern, community outreach, and "no animal testing" of its natural products. Still, inspiring a sense of "damned if you do, damned if you don't," the effort to be politically correct is disparaged as an example of how worthwhile causes are co-opted in the drive for sales and profits.

The most emphatic anti-brand critique is reserved for adidas. The German maker of athletic shoes is disparaged for outsourcing and ceasing to produce what it sells, offering extremely low wages, and its campus sponsorship activities, trying to match arch-rival Nike. In particular, the inner city "exploitation" that adidas has engaged in by sponsoring rap groups and developing lace-free shoes for street-savvy inner city kids is analyzed in detail. The fact that the initiative for the sponsorships came from inner city entrepreneurs does not seem to alleviate the consternation at the fact that there is no unmarketed "space" left for the kids. Of course, it is not so clear whether the kids themselves feel exploited, and marketers would probably applaud the effort. In fact, since there is a decided "third-world" feeling in many inner cities in America, it is only fair to acknowledge the parallel with the welcome extended to global brands in the poorer parts of the world.

The adidas brand is really not very different from its American competitors; in fact, from an anti-globalization perspective, it might be worse. The company has found itself in the midst of a world protest against its use of extra-flexible kangaroo skin for its top-of-the-line Predator soccer shoes, worn by adidas spokesperson and British superstar David Beckham. Adidas claims as much as 70% of the world market for professional soccer boots, and the success of its Predator model has been a driving force behind the killing spree on kangaroos in Australia, with both licensed and illegal hunting taking as many as seven million kangaroos a year. Animal rights groups protest the potential extinction of the kangaroo and also the nighttime killings, which, according to home movies shown on the Web site of the protesters, often involve battering kangaroo kids to death or leaving them to starve when their mothers are killed. The protest is giving rival Nike a new edge—its top-of-the-line soccer shoe, worn by another superstar, Brazilian Ronaldo, is made of 100% synthetic material.

Youth at risk?

As the short list of European brands suggests, when the product categories are similar to those of the Americans—athletic shoes, leisure apparel, beverages—the European brands are also disparaged. The practices of the Europeans are apparently not much better than those of their American competitors. One reason is clearly the diffusion of the new business model described by George Ritzer as the McDonaldization effect. Global competitive pressures tend to move these companies in similar directions in terms of operational efficiency and control, leading to third-world outsourcing, sweatshops, and low-wage labor. The luxury brands are not so much at risk, probably because their supply chains tend to be domestic, not outsourced to low-wage countries. The high prices for these products—Chanel and Vuitton bags, Cartier watches, Hermes scarves, Gucci shoes—allow production to still take place in higher wage countries, and the relatively higher creative skills required also serve to keep at least design at home. Additionally, their advertising aims at a more sophisticated clientele, and is not as in your face as the youth market ads.

If this reasoning is correct, then the anti-globalizers are not as anti-American as they might seem. The disparagement also hits European brands, when these are prominent in the same product categories as the criticized American brands. This is also consistent with another fact: The attacks are basically targeted at a select few product categories of special interest to young audiences, where globalization has meant intense competition in terms of price and promotion. It is also this same young audience that often is used to illustrate the emerging "global" world, with its McDonaldization: same clothes, same music, same movies, same sports, same problems. Anti-globalization is partly a reaction to the co-optation of this still malleable segment, targeting individuals at a time in their lives when they supposedly learn traditional values in their native culture. While marketers see the effort as an investment in brand-loyal customers for the future, others see opportunistic profiteering from the manipulation of vulnerable adolescents. And both have a point.

Anti-Globalization Limits

This analysis shows the narrow focus of the anti-globalization brand attacks to only a few product categories and market segments. Of course, there are anti-globalization protests covering a wide range of issues—the working conditions in third-world countries, environmental issues, loss of job opportunities in advanced economies—but on the market side, the issues are very circumscribed. We are talking about the reaction of the *developed* world against the invasion of a few *global brands* in *product categories* targeted mainly at *young people* and sold on the bases of *convenience, low price*, and *brand image*. The problem with these brands is that they encourage an *American lifestyle* based on superficiality and fads, all engineered by profit-seeking marketers. It is the new consumerspace with its in-your-face marketing techniques that threatens engrained ways of life and traditional culture.

Recognizing these limits of the attacks on American brands helps clarify some of the confusion surrounding the globalization debate. Globalization defenders usually point to the successes in raising third-world per-capita incomes. True enough, even though income inequality might still be a problem. They also point to the obvious successes in business-to-business markets and supply-chain efficiencies. Again correct, although here the labor conditions and environmental standards in third-world countries do become issues. Pro-globalizers also like to counter anti-branding arguments with examples of the eagerness with which these brands are welcomed in many countries. Yes, this clearly is a positive in many third-world countries. It also happens among young people in the more advanced countries. Still, especially if you are not in the target segment, many of the associated in-your-face marketing manifestations will seem intrusive, distasteful, and annoying.

So, why do the anti-globalizers get upset with such a relatively minor corner of the total marketplace? One reason is that the effects will spread. The new germs are contagious. Young people grow up under the influence of the American way of life and consumerism. They demand convenience and low prices, are insensitive to permanence, and value fashion and fads. Also, the new ways of doing marketing—and of doing business—spread to other products and other industries as businesses learn to cope with demands in the marketplace. As the McDonaldization effect suggests, the efficiency of the new business model comes to dominate other means of production and marketing.

The spread of the virus is not limited only to new ways of operations; as new methods are diffused, more and more competitors adopt these new ways to gain matching cost efficiencies and competitive advantages come gradually from market presence and dominance. This leads to a new emphasis on marketing, raising the marketing expenditures in previously staid product categories to new levels. Advertising and sales promotion efforts are ramped up as brands become increasingly important. Existing loyalties are challenged by anything from free samples and store coupons to sponsored events and saturation media campaigns.

These new developments don't necessarily emerge gradually as they might have done in the beginning, but the lifecycles are shortened and speeded up as global communications allow new audiences to quickly catch up. In fact, as foreign customs and traditions are often less puritan than those in the U.S., the content of commercials and sales pitches might be even more in your face than in America. Diesel jeans, for example, has a European campaign with two gay sailors kissing each other. A commercial for condoms in France suggests that the father of a recalcitrant kid should have used the product to save himself a lot of trouble. European commercials for American icons such as Microsoft and Levi's are now routinely too "edgy" for Americans. Leave it to the cynical Europeans to take American "in your face-ness" to new heights!

The Affluence Effect

A common pro-globalization argument is that with open market access and increasing per-capita income, countries that opt into the capitalist system can offer their consumers an increased variety of products and services. As these consumers' discretionary income rises, they grow increasingly sophisticated and demanding of quality and service. Presumably their levels of satisfaction and happiness increase as well.

This path is probably common enough, especially in emerging economies. For example, comparative studies of the Indian standard of living between the 1970s and 1990s show a markedly reduced rate of poor and homeless, improved living conditions, and an increasing middle class.[8] Although other factors are at work as well, the opening of the Indian economy to foreign investment clearly played a role. Despite the documented negatives of sweatshop conditions, child labor, and environmental degradation, globalization has helped this country raise its living standards.

In advanced countries, the picture is in many ways more complex. Better access to foreign goods is balanced by a loss of jobs in

---

8. In 1966, a Swedish researcher and a photographer documented the misery in Calcutta. Returning 33 years later, the progress was palpable. Some young Indians even disputed the photographic evidence from 1966—"things could not have been that bad." Lasse Berg and Stig T. Karlsson, *I Asiens Tid: Indien, Japan, Kina 1966-1999* (Stockholm: Ordfront), 2000, p. 42.

many industries. The increasing affluence is not evenly distributed, leading to increased inequality, and in some cases, even lower living standards (even places inside the U.S.). The greater variety of goods does not necessarily mean that quality is higher or service is better—or, for that matter, that customer satisfaction and happiness have increased.

These developments have been thoroughly documented elsewhere. However, two special features of the experience with increasing affluence should be highlighted here because they help explain why American brands might be singled out by anti-globalizers. Both are consequences of the strength of American brands in the lower end of the market. First, as consumers develop more expertise and sophistication in consumption, their tastes are likely to shift in a direction away from low-end brands. That hits American brands more. In product categories where the Americans are dominant—food and drink, apparel and shoes, entertainment and toys—increased sophistication will typically involve going away from American brands. There are exceptions, of course, but by and large, the American focus on the lower end and its younger customers means that the higher end is usually not an American strength. This helps explain why American brands are disparaged by anti-globalizers in advanced markets. They are simply less prestigious, less focused on quality, and more easily tainted by the "cheap commercialism" aura.

A second related effect is seen in the affluent American market itself. As is easily observed, American society—and the economy—are obsessed by youth. It is taken as a given that young people are the major targets of marketing efforts, the most valuable part of the television audience, and so on. One rationale is that if you get them early into your brand's "camp," they will stay with you later as they move through their lifecycle: they get married, build a house, have children, send them to college, become empty nesters, and then well-off retirees. By and large, people oblige by always staying young, always using the latest new products, always having energy, always being active. The "Always Coke" slogan is there for a reason. Being young in

America is for everyone.[9] Even the luxury market shows the effect, the new money of successful Americans likely to be spent on heavily advertised branded goods in euphoric consumerism rather than on the sedate quality-conscious sophistication one might have expected.[10] "If you've got it, flaunt it!" American brands are always dynamic, exciting, and full of life—just like its people at any age.

The sentimental image of the pioneering and resourceful American riding westward to build a new home still inspires a lot of the American brands' stress on energy, excitement, and "you-can-do-it-ness." Americans and their brands are "hot," not "cool," despite the current lingo. At least from the days of de Tocqueville, this youthful image, however beneficial in a pioneer country, has also been seen from the outside as reflecting naive optimism and unthinking self-centeredness. One shouldn't be surprised if some of the older and more sophisticated consumers in advanced economies find it easy to disparage American brands as bringers of insultingly brash commercialism.

The Commercialized Society

To sum up, American brands feature prominently in anti-globalization attacks partly because they constitute the majority (about two-thirds) of the global brands, the brands that source globally and are recognized the world over. They also show up because they are the leading brands in the product categories attacked for commercializing society with their lowest common denominator offerings—the fast-food restaurants, apparel for the teenage market, toys and entertainment, low-price convenience items. They

---

9. Gail Sheehy, whose bestselling books *Passages* (New York: Bantam Dell Doubleday, 1976) and *New Passages* (New York: Ballantine Books, 1996) first established life's turning points, argues that more recent data show a 10-year shift upward in the stages: A 50-year-old today acts like a 40-year-old used to.
10. James Twitchell's book, *Living It Up* (New York: Simon & Schuster, 2002), vividly describes the luxury consumption of Americans.

are not simply attacked because they are especially "bad" in terms of sourcing and third-world exploitation. Non-American brands also use similar sourcing strategies when in the same industries, and they also get attacked. To the extent there is an anti-American sentiment involved, it is reflected mostly in the fact that these brands represent the Americanization associated with globalization, which is again a matter of the product categories they dominate, focused on younger segments with low prices and in-your-face promotions. Since the global presence of the Europeans and especially the Japanese is weaker in these categories, they are not attacked to the same degree. In less incendiary product categories, especially in business-to-business markets, there is no sign of anti-Americanism, at least so far. We have yet to see attacks on Hewlett-Packard, Boeing, or Dell.

Will the in-your-face virus from the American brands spread to other product categories? We have seen already that it has spread to local competitors in the same categories—where it is a dog-eat-dog world—but will other sectors be infected? The evidence so far suggests a positive answer. In the U.S., an increasingly varied set of industries, from funeral parlors to computers to real-estate companies to automobiles to newspapers and television newscasts, now employ in-your-face tactics. The punditry of political commentators is more caustic than ever, as is the rhetoric of political discourse in general. It is this culture that is being exported through the American global brands, helping to create an anti-globalization backlash.

C H A P T E R

7 ANTI-AMERICANISM AND MARKETING

The big bully

"**W**hat's marketing got to do with it?" you might ask. "It" is the anti-Americanism thoroughly documented after the war in Iraq by the Pew Charitable Trust's international surveys.[1] Many commentators ascribed the negative shift in attitude toward the U.S. to the eagerness of America to go to war without a clear UN mandate. Others blamed the unilateralist rhetoric employed by the Bush administration in the period leading up to the war. Still others saw the anti-Americanism as inspired by the traditional French animosity toward the U.S. and an attempt by the Europeans to mobilize a counterbalance to the now-single superpower. But nobody really blamed American companies or their brands and their marketing practices. It was striking, in fact, to recognize that many of the anti-globalization demonstrators had shifted to an anti-war and anti-American posture, but no longer attacked American brands. Instead, the demonstrators smeared the images of Bush, Cheney, and Rumsfeld, the new icons of American power.

From a marketing perspective, the anti-Americanism seen especially in Europe looks actually as if "Brand America" is being attacked by previous allies the way global brands have been

---

1. The Pew Research Center for the People & the Press, June 2003.

disparaged by anti-globalization sympathizers. The parallels are striking. Anti-war demonstrators include many former anti-globalizers, their banners and posters denounce the faces that represent America much as the brand logos were attacked before, and putting pressure on the local politicians to reject the U.S. proposal to go to war against Iraq is similar to a demand for boycotting the global brands. Sure, more might be at stake when it comes to political and military intervention than changing buying behavior, but the logic is the same. As would be expected, the rising anti-Americanism has also spilled over into an increased rejection of American brands, although not as violent as one might have expected—the demonstrators have bigger fish to fry.

Any marketing parallels also become more salient because the American administration's spokespersons—as well as the representatives of their allies and opponents, from Tony Blair in Britain to Kofi Annan at the UN to Jacques Chirac in France and Gerhard Schroeder in Germany—all use broadcast and print media to communicate their "positions" on terrorism and war issues. Whether they like it or not, and whether or not they consciously think of it as marketing, the fact is that their use of media is tantamount to a marketing campaign to persuade their constituents—and each other—about the superiority of their offering. With President Bush having an MBA, one would expect the marketing angle to come naturally for him at least, a suspicion supported by his insistent "staying on message," similar to the way a brand's logo gets embedded in a teenager's mind by constant repetition. For better or worse, many Americans now automatically connect 9/11 to Osama Bin Laden to Sadam Hussein to WMD. As with brands, perceptions beat facts.

Marketing and 9/11

Even if at first glance the global marketing of American products and services might have little or nothing to do with rising anti-Americanism or its manifestations, a marketing perspective can be applied quite usefully in understanding and explaining anti-

Americanism. For example, it is sometimes claimed that the Bush administration's often belligerent rhetoric has exacerbated the anti-American sentiments abroad. One justification for the rhetoric is that it allegedly "plays well at home," even though it may alienate allies elsewhere. But, it also redefines "Brand America" and what it stands for at home and abroad, and one wonders if the new unilateralism and the image of a bully conjured up is sustainable in the longer run. The Bush strategy is perhaps natural, but it is also the strategy that many American multinationals were accused of pursuing in the past, when the domestic market came first and overseas markets were treated as secondary. It represents a retreat from a global perspective to an ethnocentric posture, which, judging from what happened to American multinationals in the 1970s and 1980s, will have predictably negative consequences for the U.S. itself. America is being repositioned in the wake of 9/11, becoming the world's strongest while jettisoning weak but supportive allies in the process—sort of the way the American automobile industry in the 1970s gave up the lower end of the market to concentrate on the larger cars in the home market, opening the door for the Japanese incursions.

The September 11, 2001 terrorist attacks on the World Trade Center in New York City and the U.S. Defense Department's headquarters in the Pentagon in Virginia, across the Potomac river from Washington, D.C., constitute the watershed event that has changed American international relations, perhaps forever. The surprise 9/11 attacks, which resulted in a loss of over 2,000 innocent lives, immediately generated a wave of support from traditional allies of the U.S. and most other world nations. By contrast, televised news broadcasts showed the perpetrators and their sympathizers in the Arab world celebrating the leveling of the two towers in the World Trade Center by dancing in the streets of their capitals. It was strikingly reminiscent of the "clash between civilizations" in Samuel Huntington's prescient phrase in a 1996 book of the same title.[2]

---

2.   Samuel P. Huntington, *The Clash of Civilizations and the Remaking of the World Order* (New York: Touchstone), 1996.

As America grieved, the country was galvanized under President Bush's leadership, and its military moved decisively against Osama Bin Laden and the Taliban rulers in Afghanistan. Most of the world's powers supported the invasion, and several countries sent troops. The image of the two towers of the World Trade Center burning and collapsing was a powerful symbol of evil in this world—at least for most people in the West. Presumably it was interpreted differently in Arab countries. As marketers know well, the force of an image depends on what the audience brings to it.

One of the striking facts behind the recent rise of anti-Americanism in Western countries is how quickly the supportive sympathy for America right after 9/11 has turned sour. There is no doubt that the actions and rhetoric of the Bush administration had a lot to do with this. But, we will study that later. Anti-Americanism was discernible also before 9/11, especially in the anti-globalization movement with its emphatic attacks on American brands. In addition, even though French liberal newspaper *Le Monde* proclaimed, "We are all Americans" right after the attack, this sentiment was a deviation from a more critical prior view of America, especially in France.

Anti-American sentiments had been latent in Europe and elsewhere before the anti-globalization debate. France, in particular, can be singled out as a foe, at least on the cultural side, with its insistence on linguistic purity (the official rejection of anglicized words only partly successful), subsidizing a domestic film industry so as to avoid American dominance, and having a tradition of defiance reaching back at least as far as J.J. Servan-Schreiber's *The American Challenge* from 1968 and the de Gaulle years.[3] Other countries, although not quite as insistently annoying to the Americans, also at times showed anti-American reactions. There was anti-American fallout from the Vietnam War among many socialist-leaning countries. Japanese peaceniks demonstrated in the 1980s against American nuclear-powered weapons on American bases there, in violation of the Japanese constitution. Even in

---

3.   J.-J. Servan-Schreiber, *The American Challenge* (New York: Atheneum), 1969.

West Germany, where pro-American sentiment was possibly stronger than elsewhere in post-war Europe, there were complaints about the presence of U.S. troops up through the fall of the Berlin Wall in 1989.

None of these difficulties really seemed to matter much as long as there was a need to contain the threat of communism from Soviet Russia. Differences were latent, flared up, but soon died down with some deft diplomacy on both sides. The collapse of communism, however, changed the playing field by creating one single superpower, as so many commentators have noted. Without the overriding security threat, smaller issues became more important, and the latent anti-Americanism soon infused the anti-globalization movement. In much the same way that previously suppressed ethnic and religious differences in communist Yugoslavia ignited after the fall of the Berlin Wall, countries in the more integrated EU started to assert their independence of the U.S.

During the 1990s, socialist leaders ousted moderates and assumed power in Britain, France, Germany, Sweden, and other countries. Even if the Clinton administration was able to maintain cordial relations with most, before 9/11, Europe seemed to be on its way to establishing itself as the "counter-U.S." force in the world, especially since Japan and Asia faltered. Even though Europe's combined military forces were no match for the Americans—as Europe's ineptitude in the Balkan crisis underscored—there seemed to be little need for a large army since the war against communism had been conclusively won and "The End of History" was hand, signaling the victory of liberal capitalism. One book, written just before the 9/11 attacks, bravely pronounced "The End of the American Era" and the rise of Europe.[4] Such pronouncements proved of course premature as the aftermath of 9/11 showed.

---

4. Charles A. Kupchan, *The End of the American Era* (New York: Knopf), 2002. The author served on the National Security Council during President Clinton's first term.

This gradual distancing between the U.S. and Europe during the 1990s still did not lead to a high level of anti-Americanism before President Bush took power in January 2001. Several decisions (rejection of the Kyoto Protocol, withdrawal from the International Court, raising steel tariffs and agricultural subsidies) made by Bush served to kindle the latent anti-Americanism in various countries. In the WTO, the U.S. vigorously pursued a case against Europeans for not allowing hormone-treated beef into their markets. Not all these and other similar actions were taken before the 9/11 events, but the writing was on the wall early: This President was not an internationalist in the Clinton mold, but much more focused on America as the first country. The neo-conservative notion that America needs to take on an imperial role seemed to sit well even with the early Bush administration.

The 9/11 effect

To state that the 9/11 attacks changed the situation is in a sense an overstatement. In many ways, 9/11 simply intensified the already perceptible unilateralism of the American administration. There was, to be sure, an extra layer of patriotism and religious zeal in the American agenda to punish the terrorists. If there was anything really new after 9/11, it was more in the way Europeans and other countries rallied behind the Americans, submerging any latent anti-Americanism in favor of human sympathy and expressions of support. The positive sentiment lasted at least through the autumn, as Americans attacked the Taliban in Afghanistan, chasing Osama bin Laden and his al Qaeda terrorist organization out of their strongholds there. Anti-American protests against the war on Afghanistan did take place among Arabs and in various Muslim countries. There were anti-American demonstrations in Egypt in October, attacks on Coca-Cola bottlers in Nepal in November, and anti-American protests against the war in India, Indonesia, Iran, Malaysia, Sri Lanka, and Turkey. But, by and large, through the end of the fall of 2001 and into 2002, there was little sense of anti-Americanism in the rest of the world. Even German troops, in a first since World War II, were sent abroad to join the effort in Afghanistan. By mid-June 2002, Hamed Karzai had been elected the head and political leader of Afghanistan, charged with realigning previously opposing tribal forces. While the hunt for Osama bin Laden and the al Qaeda terrorists still kept Western troops in the country, American attention had gradually shifted toward Iraq.

The start of the resurgence of anti-Americanism among Western nations can be traced to the *State of the Union* address given by President Bush on January 29, 2002. This was the "axis of evil" speech in which, suddenly and without any advance warning, Bush singled out Iran, Iraq, and North Korea as rogue nations with evil intentions against the U.S. and the West, and possessing the capability to develop nuclear weapons. This widening of the war in Afghanistan was based on a new doctrine—that of a need for pre-emptive attacks on countries believed to pose a terrorist threat to the U.S., fully articulated a few months later in a West Point graduation address by President Bush on June 1, 2002.

Anti-Americanism in the Muslim world—and increasingly elsewhere as well—intensified, further fueled by escalating conflicts between Israelis and Palestinians. On January 23, 2002, *Wall Street Journal* reporter Daniel Pearl was abducted in Karachi, Pakistan. He was found dead on February 21. Coca-Cola plants in Nepal were again attacked on January 30. While Americans staged the Salt Lake City Winter Olympics as a tribute to 9/11 victims, on March 5, South Koreans took to the streets in Seoul to protest the disqualification of a Korean athlete in a short-track skating event. In response to racist comments by Jay Leno on the *Tonight* show, McDonald's Korean Web site was bombarded with slanderous comments. On March 17, a bombing attack in the Pakistani capital Islamabad killed five people, including the wife and daughter of an American diplomat, and injured 46. On March 21, nine passersby were killed and more than 30 injured when a car bomb exploded opposite the U.S. embassy in Lima, Peru, moments before a scheduled visit by President Bush.

According to later reports, despite these expressions of anti-Americanism—or rather, under the new doctrine, *because* of them—by the summer of 2002, the American leadership had decided to attack Iraq. Recognizing that there was a need for justifying an Iraqi attack convincingly to the American people—although initially not to other nations—the administration employed the kind of persuasive media tactics common in marketing. Press conferences and media appearances were used to show evidence of the later notorious WMDs, deductions linking Iraq to the al Qaeda terrorists were put forward, and the legacy of Hussein's tyranny against his own people was documented. In only one apparent slip did Bush refer to a possible grudge against his father's enemy and purported killer—not an acceptable reason for going to war. Iraq's oil resources were not mentioned once, an omission noted by most critics. Iraq was positioned as a threat to American security, one step in the retribution for the 9/11 massacre.

At the insistence of the Secretary of State, Colin Powell, supported by most of America's traditional allies, a more or less unprovoked attack on Iraq by the U.S. was halted during early fall as the Americans sought a UN resolution for a multilateral attack. A Bush speech at the UN on the anniversary of the 9/11 attacks helped produce a consensus vote on Resolution 1441 on November 8, censoring Iraq's non-compliance with the UN's order to dismantle its arsenal. Still, the Americans were impatient with the delays as UN inspectors painstakingly probed Iraq for biological weapons and nuclear arms. Demanding a more forceful resolution in favor of an attack, on February 5, 2003, the U.S. President sent Secretary of State Powell to the UN to present evidence about the existence of these weapons in Iraq. Not convinced, and publicly stating so even before the evidence was presented, France, joined by Germany, Russia, and China, refused to support an attack resolution. The Americans decided to forge ahead anyway, and on March 21, 2003, the allied forces of the U.S. and Great Britain launched the attack on Iraq.

Tables are turned
The extraordinary U-turn in pro-American support after 9/11, within a period of a few months, is not difficult to explain. While the Afghanistan incursion was a logical retaliation against the Taliban for sheltering Osama bin Laden, the link between al Qaeda

and Iraq's Saddam Hussein was much less obvious. The Bush administration made great media efforts to sell the war to the public, stressing not only the purported 9/11 link, but also Hussein's cruelty to his own people, the lack of compliance with the earlier UN sanctions after the first Gulf War in 1991, and Hussein's covert development of biological and nuclear weapons, the notorious WMDs. While Americans seemed by and large converted (the March 10, 2003 dissent from Bush by the Dixie Chicks, a popular country music group, was followed by a public apology only four days later), the message found less resonance abroad, not only among politicians, but among people in general. Thus, although support came from the leaders of Britain, Spain, and Japan, plus several other countries—28 in total—most citizens in many of these countries were against the war. Millions of people protested around the world in March. As an exercise in IMC, the effort did not succeed. As the war began, Americans were isolated.

From a global marketer's viewpoint, the selling of the war effectively separated the home market from the global market. The communications from the administration were clearly aimed at the domestic market, not only in *what* was argued, but also *how* the arguments were presented. Flowing from the new "axis of evil" concept, the U.S. now had a moral obligation to fight evil, a message reiterated by the President in various press conferences and speeches. Couching his rhetoric in religious and moral ethos, the President suggested that God was on his side. The sacred mission, defending a fundamental principle, was difficult to reconcile with a multilateral and accommodating foreign policy. Moral absolutes are not usually negotiable. This was why the UN approach needed so much cajoling, and why the U.S. became impatient as inspections dragged on. For the home market, decisiveness had to be shown, especially with the 9/11 tie-in.

That the "rest-of-the-world" market did not acquiesce had probably more to do with the moral and religious overtones in the Bush communications than with the ultimate question about removing Hussein. Prime Minister Blair's justification for sending British troops was more succinct and along lines the Europeans might accept. Blair simply pinned the argument on Hussein's possession of biological and nuclear weapons capability as a threat to all nations. Although other leaders still favored continued inspections, Blair simply argued that time was of the essence. Compared with the muddled arguments and evidence put forward by the American administration, Blair's stand was clear and forceful. Predictably, of course, he ran into trouble when the purported weapons failed to materialize, a potentially troublesome issue the Americans' barely coherent argumentation helped to minimize.

Bush the Marketer

Was marketing partly to blame (or praise) for these developments? Did they prove that President Bush was an excellent marketer? The White House showed skillful use of marketing techniques ("stay on message" against terrorism, patriotic photo opportunities for the press, and so on), but then why gamble away the goodwill abroad after 9/11? There were, of course, clear marketing principles involved in the process. Marketing considerations help define what language to use when formulating policy statements. The rhetoric used by Bush, however clipped and mangled, seemed carefully crafted in this manner. Marketing considerations also dictate the appropriate occasion and audience. Again, the Bush occasions were clearly orchestrated well. And the policy marketed—the "product," as it were—seemed partly dictated by marketing considerations. No complexities, but simply black and white, designed to appeal to the audience emotions of 9/11, and tailored to the verbal abilities of its purveyor.

President Bush is certainly not the first American president to use marketing and marketers in office. President Clinton used opinion polling extensively before major policy presentations, as did the first Bush. Market research has also been part and parcel of political campaigns for a long time. Many research agencies—Gallup, Harris, Yankelovich, and so on—routinely tap into voter sentiment for the major newspapers in any given election year, and several focus group agencies in Washington, D.C. specialize in political campaign research.

In President Bush's administration, marketing thinking and strategy have undoubtedly become more pervasive. The driving force in this is said to be his political adviser Karl Rove, previously a manager of his own direct marketing firm. Rove remains behind the scenes and without cabinet standing to exert considerable influence on the President. He is apparently the main marketing strategist in the White House.

Some well-known and obvious examples exemplify this marketing influence. Although a risky strategy because of the association with ignorance and arrogance, President Bush's appearances try to leverage his natural affinity with the strong and self-reliant cowboy image used so successfully in the Marlboro cigarette ads. He uses photo ops against the four presidential profiles on Mount Rushmore, walking alone on a red carpet to a press conference, and the notorious plane landing on the carrier *Abraham Lincoln*. The timing and setting of public announcements are also carefully planned. The rejection of the Kyoto Protocol on global warming was announced by a lower level bureaucrat in the Department of Environmental Protection, not the White House. The later resignation of the head of the Environmental Protection Agency, Christine Todd-Whitman, was announced on a late Friday afternoon, the traditional Washington "hour of massacres." The 2004 Republican Convention was scheduled for "Ground Zero" at the World Trade Center in New York City to keep alive and capitalize on the terrorist threat. In the run-up to the Iraq war, press conferences became the medium for steady repetition of the charges against Saddam Hussein and the terrorist threat, biological warfare, and WMDs—all against a backdrop of 9/11. Bothersome queries about the plans for Iraq reconstruction, the cost of the war, the strength of the links to Al Qaeda, and the lack of evidence for the notorious WMDs went largely unheeded and unanswered as the marketing strategists tried to avoid diffusing the policy's positioning.

Seen in this light, Secretary of State Powell's insistence on consulting the UN clearly presented a marketing problem, and was treated as such by most in the administration and outside, including Newt Gingrich in his speech claiming that the State

Department had not aligned itself with the President's program.[5] The State Department had in fact hired a marketing consultant in the fall of 2002, well-known positioning and advertising expert Jack Trout. Author of several books on the art of positioning as "owning" a piece of a customer's brain, and also a proponent of art as warfare, Trout was hired to train new diplomats in the art of projecting a positive image of America overseas. This was part of a larger program, "Brand America," launched by the government after September 11, 2001. Trout was working with Charlotte Beers, Under-Secretary of State for Public Diplomacy and Public Affairs, herself an advertising veteran, having held the top job at both the J. Walter Thompson and Ogilvy & Mather ad agencies. She managed a public relations program of "shared values," an effort to film the personal stories of successful immigrants to the U.S. Then videotapes were sent to foreign television stations for broadcast, a vain effort given the belligerence of the administration.

By March 2003, when the consulting ended and Trout was free to speak, he talked about the experience. Not one to mince words, Trout criticized the positioning of "Brand America" as the world's last superpower "the world's worst branding idea."[6] During his consulting stint in the State Department, he tried to shift the unilateral rhetoric used to a more encompassing position that would resonate worldwide. In Trout's view, the problem was not the policy itself, but its presentation. The language used suggested that an Iraq war was an American prerogative, a position later undermined as Bush sought UN support for a multilateral agreement. In the eyes of Trout and other branding experts, Bush had called for a repositioning of "Brand America," a significant shift and difficult to pull off.

---

5. Edward Walsh and Juliet Eilperin, "Familiar Blast, Then Unfamiliar Silence; Gingrich Lying Low After Attack on State Dept. Leaves Some Conservatives Fuming," *The Washington Post*, April 26, 2003, p. A04.
6. Deb Monroe, "Jack Trout, Author of 'Big Brands Big Trouble,' Is Concerned That the International Marketing of America Is Being Handled Improperly," *Marketplace*, March 28, 2003.

Repositioning "Brand America"

The basic idea behind all branding campaigns is to communicate a clear message that people come to associate with the brand and that elicits specific emotional attachments. In this sense, the original message after 9/11 was good branding strategy: "Punish the terrorists responsible for the attacks, and protect America from future acts of terror." One potential, but seemingly minor, problem was perhaps the second part of the message, which seemed to lack concern for other countries. But in the immediate aftermath of the attacks, when most other countries pledged support for America ("We are all Americans"), the message seemed appropriate and effective.

After the "axis of evil" speech by Bush to the Congress in January 2002, the branding message changed and the "Brand America" position diffused. First, there was a need for connecting Iraq to the terrorists, something requiring considerable communication efforts that still, as we know, failed to convince all audiences. But the greater damage to the brand might have been the decidedly unilateral rhetoric used to sell the broadened concept of the brand. America was taking on the rogue nations of the world in an effort to preserve its own security, and other countries had better watch out. As Tracey Riese, another branding consultant from New York, said, "Our branding failed to display any concern for people around the world. Instead of placing it in the context of *everyone* wanting to feel safe, it was still about *our* desire to feel safe." "Brand America" was simply interested in its own people—it had defined its target market as America, pure and simple. Previously supportive foreign countries were rejected unilaterally, and not surprisingly, turned more or less anti-American.

To some people, the Bush White House is ruining "Brand America." It is repositioning a brand that once stood for equality and tolerance of different peoples and freedom for all into a brand that stands for prejudice against foreigners, pride in its strength, and belligerence against outsiders. This strategy has played extraordinarily well among many Americans, with the 9/11 attacks used as a backdrop to repeat the implicit message that foreign countries cannot be trusted and are not worth caring about. Fueled by frequent reminders from Bush of the most fatal foreign attack ever on U.S. soil, the American people apparently are still thirsty for revenge for 9/11 to an extent less hot-heads—and many foreigners—do not appreciate. The new attacks by terrorists in other parts of the world—Bali, Saudi Arabia, Djakarta, even Baghdad—only render validity to Bush's claims (although one wonders whether there would be less attacks without the war on Iraq). Thus, focusing the message on American security serves to bolster the President's standing in his own country—and in his re-election campaign—precisely because foreign countries are antagonized. Seen in this way, disparaging France and the French is simply a marketing tactic.

Stretching too far?

The more fundamental question in the Bush marketing campaign is whether the repositioning of "Brand America" goes against the very core values that the brand stands for. The unilateralism, abrasiveness, arrogance, religious zeal, lack of humility, and self-righteousness evidenced in some of the pronouncements from the administration comprise really bad marketing considering what "Brand America" once stood for. Marketers, as Jack Trout says, would predict failure. In marketing, the solution to this problem is to introduce a secondary brand, the way Levi's introduced Dockers when it wanted to appeal to the more adult market. For Bush, a similar strategy would suggest something along the lines of "Texamerica" to signal the core propositions of the new brand.

Some observers, notably Naomi Klein, have also questioned the use of marketing techniques to position a "Brand America." Their argument is that positioning a brand requires simple and clear messages about the core values of the brand. There should be little room for alternative interpretations of what these values stand for and what the brand represents. Two of the most basic values in America are liberty and diversity. What these values mean is that America is a messy place, with lots of different people from different countries, with different ideas about religion, family life, and culture. According to these observers, the variety makes it difficult to treat America as a brand in the marketing sense. There is none of the homogeneity, the standardization, the careful tailoring of logos that one would expect with a brand—and which, not incidentally, one can see in the White House's marketing efforts.

As a marketer, I would contend that even a "messy and diverse" country can also be a brand. "Messy and diverse" are simply the core values of the brand. The fact that it represents different things to different people is not by itself a reason for rejecting it as a true brand. The Ford brand is viewed differently by people in different countries, as is Budweiser beer. Naomi Klein still has a point: One would like the target segment members to share a certain positive image of the brand. This is why one can argue that Bush has simply targeted the American home market, where the new image plays well. The new image also alienates foreigners, and perhaps some Americans, for whom the "messy and diverse" image is preferable. As a marketer, one cannot help remembering how "New Coke" was overturned by a grassroots movement to bring back "Classic Coke." Will history repeat itself?

Brand spillover

The rapid turnaround toward anti-American sentiments has naturally raised questions about what might happen to American businesses—and brands—abroad. Observers differ in the degree to which they think political disagreements will carry over into economics and business. While some businesspeople argue that the two are separate and will continue to be so, many experts, notably Jeffrey Garten, Dean of Yale University's School of Management, are not so sanguine. According to Garten, some fallout is inevitable, although it is too early to say what form it will take.[7] The sentiment is echoed by John Quelch, a Senior Associate Dean and marketing professor at Harvard Business School, who worries about the long-term loss of American brands' appeal and

---

7. Jeffrey Garten, "A Foreign Policy Harmful to Business, *Business Week*, October 14, 2002, p. 72.

market share as foreign consumers' emotional attachment to the brands vanishes.[8]

Given this, it is not surprising to learn from survey statistics that political and military developments have spilled over into increased distaste for American brands overseas. In a March 2003 survey by the Leo Burnett advertising agency, in India, China, South Korea, Indonesia, and the Philippines, one out of four people in the Asia-Pacific region said they have avoided purchasing American brands.[9] German bicycle-maker Riese und Mueller cancelled all business deals with American suppliers. Some restaurants in Hamburg and elsewhere in Germany have banned Coke and Marlboro cigarettes and won't accept the American Express card any longer.

On the home front, Americans have been venting their frustrations by bashing foreign brands. After the lack of support for Secretary of State Powell after his presentation of evidence against Iraq at the UN, the front page of the *New York Post*, a conservative newspaper, denounced the French and German foreign ministers as "weasels" who evaded commitment to a staunch ally. The conservative Fox News TV channel flashed banners with "weasels" and "vultures" associated with France and Germany. The cafeteria in the Congress on Capitol Hill changed its "French fries" to "Freedom fries," and the Speaker of the House proposed an anti-Beaujolais campaign. A Florida bar owner dumped French and German wines into the gutter to protest the countries' anti-war stand.[10] Americans boycotted French restaurants and cancelled planned trips to France. In the second quarter of 2003, French wine sales to America dropped 24% compared with the same period the year before.[11]

---

8. Richard Tomkins, "Anti-war Sentiment Is Likely to Give Fresh Impetus to the Waning Supremacy of US Brands, *Financial Times*, March 27, 2003, p. 19.

9. Normandy Madden, "Survey: Brand Origin Not Major Factor for Most Asians," *Advertising Age,* April 7, 2003, p. 33.

10. Maxine Chen and Bridget Harrison, "Protester Has a Gripe with Grape," *The New York Post*, March 8, 2003, p. 3.

11. *The Economist*, July 5, 2003, p. 43.

Even luxury brands were not immune. For example, in April 2003, BMW's American sales fell 10% after 15 months of continuous increases and Mercedes' sales fell for the first time since October, dropping 6.8%.[12] Although a weakening dollar played some part, the German lack of support for Bush clearly played a role as well.[13]

A March 2003 survey by *Brandweek*, a branding magazine, polled 12,300 Americans to find out what they thought about American and foreign brands. The respondents overwhelmingly supported brands that were perceived as representing "lasting and solidly American values," and downgraded brands that were foreign or simply perceived to be foreign. The top ten brands were: Coca-Cola, Avis, Wal-Mart, KeySpan, AOL.com, Pepsi, AT&T Wireless, Major League Baseball, Sears, and Amazon.com. Foreign beer brands, including German Beck's, Heineken, and Corona, were dead last among 180 brands. A sizable 82% of respondents supported the notion that advertising for American brands should continue in wartime, but preferably with patriotic themes (62%).[14]

As a brief media examination from both sides of the Atlantic makes clear, the emotional intensity of the reactions to the Iraq war differs between Europe and the U.S. In Europe, the argument against a war was basically a rational-legal one, that is, the evidence against Hussein was not strong enough to justify a preemptive strike. The American case for a war was basically emotional, primarily the desire to avenge the 9/11 attacks, but also a need to stand up against evil and protect America. This emotional base was unfortunately difficult to defend in rational and logical terms without stretching the available evidence pretty thin. Bush being no Hamlet, the desire to act apparently overwhelmed the need for further thought.

---

12. Michael Ellis, "German Carmakers Hit by Backlash or Weak Dollar?" *Forbes.com*, May 5, 2003.

13. Aliza Marcus, "Anti-war Europeans Target U.S. Brands Coke, McDonald's, Others Boycotted," *The Boston Globe*, March 27, 2003, p. C1.

14. From *Brandweek*, March 31, 2003.

The Fallout

In the end, it is not surprising that the rise of anti-American sentiment in many ways resulted from marketing-like efforts. First, latent anti-Americanism was reflected in the anti-globalization demonstrations, directed specifically against American businesses and brands as the most obvious beneficiaries of open and free markets. After 9/11, anti-American sentiment turned positive and supportive. But as U.S. attention shifted from the united Afghanistan effort to Iraq, the accompanying unilateral and preemptive rhetoric served to alienate the cooler leaders of previous allies. Anti-Americanism abroad rose to the new heights documented by the Pew surveys. Presumably not intended by Bush, the new anti-Americanism was a by-product of the selling of the war to the American people, in what is likely to become a classic attempt to reposition "Brand America."

As many commentators have suggested, the new anti-Americanism reflects, unavoidably, a kind of anti-Bush sentiment abroad. It is not uncommon to hear statements such as, "We are not against America, but against Bush." In Japan, newspaper columnists have rechristened Rumsfeld the "Secretary of Offense." These sentiments suggest that the repositioning of "America"—the confrontational rhetoric and belligerent stance—does not go well with America's past image of ethnic diversity and religious tolerance. It is natural to assume that the change is only temporary, that America will come back to its roots, and "Brand America" will return to its former position. But for this, there might have to be a change in the U.S. Presidency and administration. In fact, some anti-globalizers in Europe have asked their supporters to mute their anti-Americanism for fear of strengthening Bush's case.

When Bush speaks, he naturally evokes that moral conviction and emotional sentimentality which have now become the staple not only of Hollywood movies, but of Washington political rhetoric. "Brand America" currently packs an emotional wallop that surely is stronger than ever. Nobody is against our President, our troops, our way of life. Nobody, that is, except foreigners. Foreigners, beware! As the President has it, if Iraqis mess with American soldiers, "Bring 'em on." Our soldiers are "plenty tough." This is, of course, effective brand-building communications given 9/11. But, it's a rhetoric fit for some beleaguered Fort Apache, not for the sole superpower in the world. There is nothing heroic about U.S. drone bombers taking on Saddam Hussein's Republican Guard.

As for the effect on American business and brands, it's good to remember that the presence of foreign products and brands is in many ways the most visible manifestation of international relations and trade. For most people, political and economic developments take place on TV or in the newspaper. We are simply observers on the sidelines. But products are more tangible to us and therefore more real. Products also show up on TV commercials and in newspaper ads in most countries. A negative perception of American leadership and its intentions as portrayed in the media is easily transferred to a negative perception of an American brand. This is not complicated or unusual. It can happen to other countries' leaders and products as well, especially when emotions and sentiment dominate decision-making. American talk-show hosts feel free to express their political views by bashing foreign brands. President Bush leads the way, by inviting supportive foreign leaders to White House dinners and uninviting those less supportive. Economic aid and trade deals are given to countries supporting the war, not to others. American participation in the 2003 Paris Air Show was severely limited, and American wine merchants were conspicuously absent at the annual Bordeaux Wine Fair in 2003.[15] Americans are hot about the war effort—largely because of the 9/11 tie-in—and if the Europeans took them seriously, these retaliations could easily get out of hand. So far they don't. But, we shouldn't expect other people to be more tolerant and patient than we are.

---

15. Craig S. Smith, "U.S. Chill Flattens Mood at French Wine Fair," *The New York Times*, June 30, 2003, p. 3.

8 WHO WANTS TO BE AMERICAN?

A promised land?

America, because of its geographical size and distance from other continents, has never been a great tourist destination. Even U.S. citizens find it difficult to squeeze in Mount Rushmore and the Grand Canyon on the same itinerary. Overseas visitors have additional problems. The aftermath of the 9/11 attacks, with its sense of insecurity at home and heightened readiness at the borders, has not made for a very reassuring or welcoming image for foreign tourists. Air travel is more cumbersome than ever. As for prospective immigrants, the war in Iraq and the ensuing loss of goodwill overseas have undoubtedly made some people hesitate. For those forging ahead, the closer scrutiny and security measures in American embassies and consulates over-seas become obstacles that increase the risk of denial. Sure, illegal immigrants from the south still try to enter, but also at greater risk. Fewer people want to come, and Americans don't want them.

The figures for tourists entering the U.S. for the first quarter of 2003 show a decline of 7.6% from the corresponding period in 2002, for a first quarter drop of 588,000 visitors. In March alone, the war month, the decline was 20.3%.[1] This drop is not

---

1. Data from Office of Travel and Tourism Industries, *http://tinet.ita.doc.gov/*.

merely due to lack of interest on the part of would-be visitors. In May, the State Department announced the beginning of face-to-face interviews with most foreign nationals who want a visa to travel to the U.S. The application fee was increased to $100, non-refundable, on top of which a visa fee may be added. The message is pretty clear: Don't come!

Of course, this is not a one-way street. Americans now travel less not only inside their country, but also overseas. Europe, France, and Germany in particular, have seen sharp drop-offs in American tourists. But even a country like Spain, with official—if not popular—support for the war in Iraq, has suffered. The number of Americans traveling to Spain, typically somewhere over one million in a season, fell by almost 20% in 2002, and by another 19.5% in the first four months of 2003. The erosion of the dollar's value is partly responsible, but much of the reason is attributable to the antipathy the Americans expect in Europe.[2]

Destination America

Tourism is of course not the only, and probably not even the best, indicator of a country's relationship with the rest of the world. But the figures are striking because they reflect not just the security risks associated with terrorism, but also the kind of confrontational attitude and behavior evidenced by the American administration. Does the unattractiveness of America and the Americans' lack of travel interest bear any relationship to the belligerent and unilateralist rhetoric of Bush? This is very likely. Predictably, elsewhere in America, there is evidence of these things. The foreign students who tend to flock to American colleges, especially at the graduate level, apparently have started to consider alternatives at home or elsewhere. For example, a good percentage of the MBAs that we educate in the business schools in the U.S. are foreign nationals; here at Georgetown, they typi-

---

2. John Tagliabue, "Americans Ever More Scarce in Tourist-Popular Spain," *The New York Times*, May 22, 2003, p. W1.

cally number around 30%. Their presence is financially important to the universities because they tend to pay full tuition and have fewer opportunities to qualify for an American scholarship than U.S. citizens. Now prospective MBAs of Brazil and other places are looking to Europe, to France, Britain, and Spain for their education.[3]

Why are these facts important? There is a simple reason: For most people, whether pro- or anti-globalization, the most realistic vision of the land promised by globalization is the U.S. The U.S. is not only one of the most economically advanced countries in the world after the collapse of communism, it is also the strongest military and political nation. When people are asked to "become global," the American way of life is probably what they visualize. What this country looks like, what it represents, and how others think of it are all important issues that not only show evidence of anti-Americanism, but, in the bigger picture, whether globalization will have a chance to succeed in bringing a better life to people.

Most pro-globalization economic writings seem to have in mind an ultimate destination where the free flows in merchandise trade, investment, and people have made countries grow and everybody better off—a sort of economic Nirvana, reached via open markets, deregulation, and ideally, privatization. Sure, the destination cannot be reached overnight, and there will be some traveling pains, but with patience and determination, the goal will be reached. Think of the great wagon trails going through the American West, with the experts at the WTO, the World Bank, and the IMF riding as Indian scouts.

Judging from the many lost skirmishes in various countries in the past few years, the pro-globalization caravan is not delivering on the vision without a lot of traveling pain. Many countries have found their currency and budget problems alone sufficient to strike camp before going further. They may not be backtracking to the old sites yet, but they are not sure whether it is worth trek-

---

3. Tony Smith, "Allure of Europe Is Drawing Students," *The New York Times*, July 18, 2003, pp. W1, W7.

king any further west. El Dorado may be beckoning, but it could just be a chimera. Argentina's troubles in the wake of its 2001 release of the peg to the U.S. dollar and the ensuing peso devaluation is only one of the most blatant examples of IMF policy advice gone wrong.

As always with these kinds of adventures, the willingness to pursue the goal depends on several things, like the strength of the vision. How good is life there, really? How nice can it be? Another is the travail of the journey. How painful is the trip? What are the sacrifices? Then there is the sureness of the path. How certain are we that the map will lead us there? Will we be lost in the wilderness? These concerns are set against the fact that many in the party will have a place to lose; they are leaving home.

On every count, the anti-globalization forces score points. The vision is not spotless. The pain seems out of proportion to the gain. The scouts disagree about the best way to get there. And, with the nostalgia that time and distance awakens, "It was nicer before."

A shining city?

Taking stock of life in America at the beginning of the new millennium is not difficult for anybody, wherever they are. In most newspapers and broadcast media around the world, economic and political news from America provides an anchor and benchmark for one's own country's achievements and failures. To beat America in the neverending statistical contests between nations is a particularly potent source of satisfaction. Recently, anti-Americanism has tended to kindle these fires to new heights.

People note that UN's Human Development Index (HDI)—a composite measure of life expectancy, education, and income per person—shows that in 2002, the U.S. ranked "only" sixth, after Norway, Sweden, Canada, Belgium, and Australia.[4] The gender empowerment indicator, which measures the degree to which

---

4.   http://hdr.undp.org/reports/global/2002/en/.

women participate in political decision-making, places the U.S. in the 11th position. The U.S. Department of Labor shows that hourly compensation for production workers in manufacturing still lags behind most of Europe and Japan, as it has for most of the 1990s. U.S. literacy rates are relatively low, although that's partly because of the high level of immigration, the U.S. accepting by far the largest contingents of new people every year, somewhere around a million annually (in 2002, there were 1,063,732 legal immigrants, to which can be added an untold number of illegal immigrants).[5] American public schools are not as deficient as they used to be, but U.S. math proficiency is still no match for most of Europe, and of course, Asia.

And, these are the more positive statistics. When it comes to social negatives such as divorce, crime rate, and, in particular, violent crime, the U.S. often leads the pack. Even the steady pro-globalization *The Economist*, presumably alarmed at the smudge on the vision, devoted the front page and main feature of a 2002 issue to a story about the many convicts in American prisons. Measuring the prison rate in terms of number of convicts per 100,000, the U.S. leads the world at 700, followed closely at 670 by Russia, a notoriously lawless society after the fall of the Berlin Wall. Figures for European countries such as France and Italy are at around 100, while Japan, despite a hike during the post-bubble 1990s, comes in at 48.[6]

Statistics do not show the complete picture, of course. The land of the free and home of the brave is presumably still the most dynamic entrepreneurial economy in the world, with more opportunity for motivated and ambitious people than any other country. In fact, as we have seen, although the terrorist attacks on 9/11 dealt a blow to economic progress, they also induced a kind of resurgence of the American spirit, this time in terms of

---

5.   *2002 Yearbook of Immigration Statistics*, Bureau of Citizenship and Immigration Services, p. 5.

6.   *The Economist*, August 10–16, 2002, pp. 25–27. It should be noted that a significant percentage of U.S. inmates are in prison for various drug offenses, which might not result in imprisonment in other countries.

politics and military might rather than economics. If some people in the past had doubts about the strength and vitality of American society, they are now to be convinced with means other than trade and investments. As the U.S. policies persist, anti-globalization forces become stronger and more anti-American than ever. For now, not only are there cracks in the picture of the shining city, it also seems to be clad in armor. As Americans surely should know after crafting all those persuasive World War II anti-Nazi movies, the key to winning a war is to win people's hearts and minds, not bully them into submission.

Universal values: pro and con

American values are assuredly universal. They form the basis on which the founding fathers wrote the invitation to welcome all people. Benjamin Franklin was right to emphasize the moral basis on which the country's policies, including foreign policy, were founded. The inalienable "freedom to pursue one's own happiness" still manifests itself in Americans' day-to-day lives. The idea of America as the "land of opportunity" often seems to refer only to the availability of the immense natural resources in this land of plenty, but a prerequisite is its embodiment in the articles of the Constitution, inspiring each individual's effort by protecting his or her right to material gains.

This is what makes America so attractive to people around the world, and they might come—unless, of course, they have the material possessions and success already. The pull of America is particularly strong for people from poor countries, and America is also a haven for refugees escaping racial, ethnic, and political persecution. But not all foreigners are "poor and down-trodden." America is not so attractive to people from advanced countries, especially those who are successful in their home countries and who therefore have to give up something to come here. I don't know how clear this is to Americans, but for an immigrant like myself, it is a central fact of my life. As so many immigrant novels describe in eloquent prose, the choices one makes can come back to haunt you.

What one gives up when leaving one's home country after a certain age—the culture and traditions, yes, but more the comfortable understanding of habits and unspoken words, of people's gestures and ways of doing things, of daily life and what to do on weekends, and so on—is primarily the knowledge of how to live well and accomplish things given one's environment. "Familiarity" is the common word for it.

I know this sounds minor and inconsequential. But it has some practical consequences for various things, including business management and the things we teach in the business school. I'll give you an example: When a Swedish-born store manager for IKEA, the multinational furniture-maker out of Sweden, spoke to my MBA class, she was asked what the key to success as an IKEA manager was. After some reflection and some back and forth with the students, the class, and reluctantly the manager, concluded that "being Swedish" was the key—and this in one of the most multinational of companies. The reason: For effective coordination, the global organization needed the implicit understanding (the "tacit knowledge" we call it) that comes with being from the same culture.

This is the understanding that familiarity with a home country culture yields. It makes for a much more comfortable and peaceful life. You can find it in European countries, and in spades in Japan. Since I am an immigrant here, I am not really in a position to judge what it's like to be an American, but I doubt that a country that values individual freedom, energy, challenge, and diversity to the extent America does can offer much peace and tranquility to its citizens.

American values are universal for good reason: The country needs to accommodate a wide variety of people from different cultures. But while this is commendable and attractive in principle, the downside is that such an all-inclusive bond between the people cannot be used to settle very many issues in day-to-day life. If all are equal, and have equal rights to free access, and are empowered to pursue their own dreams, it is hard to build a strong community where some people might have to yield to others (we can't all park our cars in same slot; we might have trouble deciding which church to build; all sports might not be supported, etc.). I don't need to emphasize this since we all know it, but it is simply hard to work as a team when everybody comes from a different background and all have their own ideas and desires. Most civilized people recognize this and make some accommodation for others (or go further West). Even so, however, when the team gets together, we have to make sure everybody understands what their role is and what the expectations are. American business managers, not surprisingly, spend a lot of time explaining things that seem obvious to people from more homogeneous cultures.

Freedom debased

"Freedom" is perhaps the value most closely associated with America. The country was founded as a haven of freedom for many oppressed people, immigrants to the new country. The language of freedom forms the oratory of the country's presidents, from Washington to Lincoln to Kennedy and now Bush. Martin Luther King's "I have a dream" speech on the Washington Mall in 1963 ends with a "Free at last" coda to great effect. When I was at Berkeley, the "free speech movement" made headlines by confronting—in the end successfully—the university's ban on political action on campus. Of the many alleged reasons for the war in Iraq, the only one unchallenged is that it would free Iraqi citizens from oppression.

So, how has America fared with its own freedom? Not so well, in my estimation, and I think us marketers have to accept some blame. When I came to the U.S. in 1964, I found America not a good country, but in a way a great country. A "good" country seemed to me a country where the citizens treated each other with courtesy and respect, where people listened to each other, where the poor were provided for, where healthcare and living conditions met minimal standards, and where differences were settled by reason more than emotion. I didn't find much of this "good country" in America back then (of course, coming from well-organized Sweden with its welfare system might have biased my view). But it was kind of a "great" country because people were alive and friendly; they were terrific in practical matters such as helping to fix the fanbelt in your car, helping to find a dentist, or organizing a garage sale when you moved. And it seemed that practical matters were everywhere and everything. What to do was the question; actions spoke louder than words. Even in the free speech movemeunt, organizing a demonstration and deciding where to hold the post-party seemed at least as important as the ideas. Even if the country was not very good, and really not well-organized I thought, individual people were great on their own. And people were good at having a good time.

I am not so positive anymore, of course. I think the lack of social cohesion and reliance on individual freedom have pushed the country much too far in a bad direction. A free country now seems to mean that you have to take care of your own, you don't bother with other people, there is no need to apologize, you do what you have to do, and you don't expect much of others. I would say that the freedom given to individuals and to large corporations has moved the country away from its promise of a better society. The individual utility-maximizing choices have accumulated and brought the country down in a kind of "race to the bottom." The in-your-face complaints in this book are really only special cases of the general malaise. America has not stayed true to its promise. The America of *Affluenza* and crime, divorce, and other various social ailments—to which now can be added hubris and belligerence—make one wonder how the freedom so highly valued has come to be so badly corrupted.

Freedom vs. virtue
In the debate surrounding the terrorist threat from Islam extremists, a distinction is typically made between freedom and virtue. While Western societies following Judeo-Christian traditions emphasize freedom, Islam stresses virtue. Leading a virtuous life, that is, living according to Koran scripture, is the highest aim for an individual. Western writers counter that a life lived under the constraints of the Muslim clergy and autocratic rulers in many Islamic countries can hardly be judged virtuous.

Without free choice, there is no virtue—good behavior is enforced.[7]

The proponents of freedom argue that making choices as free men and women is a prerequisite for a more noble and virtuous society. It is also a Christian tenet that God gave men free will. However, my own sense is that the Americans surely are free, but they have used this freedom to become less virtuous than one might have hoped. I also think that the in-your-face marketing efforts discussed elsewhere in this book have helped derail many good intentions.

There are virtuous Americans to be sure. According to published data, Americans tend to give more to charities and worthy causes than many other people. The figure for 2002 was $240 billion.[8] The country still accepts more than its share of the world's poor and downtrodden. The U.S. is now the leading government donor in the world, its $10.9 billion in foreign aid in 2001 beating out Japan's $9.7 billion.[9] High schools require students to do voluntary work in their communities. Individual professionals, such as medical doctors, set aside time during the year when they perform pro bono work for the needy. Soup kitchens, drug rehabilitation centers, and school luncheon crews are staffed by volunteers.

Still, I hesitate to be too optimistic. Many of the individuals who donate funds for various causes have remaining assets that are stunningly large. Many others with similar assets don't give unless the tax benefits are great enough. Self-preservation instincts are necessarily strong. As border controls have stiffened in the wake of the terrorist attacks, immigrants face a much less welcoming attitude. The U.S. official aid to foreign countries may be large in total, but as a percentage of GDP, the aid, at 0.1 percent, ranks *last* among the world's wealthiest countries. And many of the volunteers are needed because federal and state funding of various

---

7.   A nice version of this argument is in Dinesh D'Souza's article, "The Power of Virtue," *The Washington Post*, July 4, 2003, p. A23.

8.   The 2003 "Giving USA" report, *www.GivingUSA.org*.

9.   Data from the Council of Foreign Relations.

programs is so low. While many other countries use tax money to fund various educational and social programs, the U.S. leaves these programs to rely on the uncertainty of individual goodwill and volunteerism. Maintaining freedom for individuals to be virtuous can mean that public schools and social programs are not funded adequately.

Another discouraging aspect of the level of virtue in America is the number of cases where individual freedom has had to be constrained by mandated regulations. These can be called failures of freedom, if you want. An obvious but perhaps unfair example is the recent introduction of homeland security alerts, with their increased police surveillance, stepped-up airport checks, and exhortations to "report suspicious persons or activities." One would hope the Patriot Act to be temporary, despite the political rhetoric emphasizing the danger.

Other examples of regulations are more striking—even to Europeans, I suspect, even though their governments are supposedly much more friendly to regulation than the American government. Take the smoking ban in the U.S., for example. Not only is your own office off-limits, so are whole buildings and even restaurants and bars. We apparently can't trust individuals to avoid blowing smoke on others. And the cigarette companies are having a tough time of it, having to pay for luring so many free individuals into smoking. The lack of corporate responsibility suggests that the rejected lawsuit against McDonald's for serving dangerous food is likely to surface again in some form. Affirmative action, recently re-affirmed, helps us deal with the problems of minorities. What happened to virtuous tolerance? Gays are now allowed some privacy—by law. Why was this necessary? Gun control, however, is still basically off–limits. Here, we can apparently be trusted, despite all the evidence of not-so-virtuous behavior.

For future generations?
It is not just the vision of globalization's promised land that has been smudged, but the path that leads to it is increasingly painful and uncertain. The path involves sacrifices in the form of fiscal discipline (by which the IMF means "don't run a deficit"), hard

work (that is, "work as hard as Americans"), and patience ("delayed gratification"—not something we marketers endorse). By and large, people are asked to work for future generations, but can only hope to generate some gradual improvement along the way. Exactly how much and when benefits will come is not clear—and nobody really seems to know for sure whether anything will actually materialize in the short run. For many, including Russia, Argentina, and Indonesia, the first few steps go down rather than up.

As marketers know, motivating people by referring to their children can be very powerful. Kindling fears of not being able to reach your teenage daughter at night has sold many cell phones. More positively, one argument for European Community membership has been the notion that one's children could go to college anywhere in Europe. If one wants a good pro-globalization rationale, refer to opportunities for the next generation.

Of course, there are limits to how far even the most dedicated parent will go. This becomes even more of an issue once there is doubt about the path itself. This doubt arises easily when it seems one has taken one step forward but two steps back, as many countries have experienced. By and large, the globalization path is not very sure, now less than ever if recent World Bank publications are to be believed. When there is some gradual reinforcement by recognizable improvements, most people will be happy to do their share. In fact, judging from what we know about human psychology, one would expect that the fun is in the journey, more than in the arrival. When the Japanese economy was growing in the 1960s and 1970s, people were still poor but hopeful and positive, sentiments replaced by wealth and arrogance in the 1980s and early 1990s. The inspiring stories we read tend to be about the exhilaration of people going somewhere or accomplishing something, less about being there—think of Steve Jobs and the first Mac, of Winston Churchill in World War II, of Thor Heyerdahl and Kon-Tiki. Once the goal has been reached and the mountain has been climbed, is satisfaction guaranteed? Hardly—there are ever more peaks to climb and goals to be won as aspiration levels rise. Economics is, after all, the science of the dismal. The shining city might always be just beyond our reach.

Winner take all?

Another obstacle in globalization's path to America is the question of who ends up with all the economic benefits. Pro-globalization writers rightly point to the growth in various socioeconomic indicators. Compared to the status quo, there will be increases in per-capita income, export volume, infrastructure development, literacy rates, and so on. Some of these aggregate statistics are incontrovertible—less illiteracy, better schooling, and improved healthcare are good things in most places, although it is not clear that only globalization is at work here. In other cases, globalization does indeed seem to be a key factor in sustaining a healthy growth rate, but the aggregate numbers hide the fact that the gains are not always very evenly distributed across the population.

The data on income distribution in various countries suggest overall that the progress of globalization has been accompanied by a corresponding increase in income inequality. Even if "all boats rise with the tide," which is not at all a certainty, some have risen much higher than others. Not the least striking is the fact that the inequality has become particularly pronounced in the U.S. If the rest of the world's countries are to become "more like us," the evidence suggests that there is to be more income inequality than before.[10] In the U.S., a popular bestseller has proclaimed the coming of the "winner-take-all society."[11] This is pretty distressing for many people, especially when the way

---

10. The most recent government data show that in the U.S., the gap between rich and poor more than doubled from 1979 to 2000. In 2000, the richest 1% of Americans had more money to spend after taxes than the poorest 40%. Lynnley Browning, "U.S. Income Gap Widening, Study Says," *The New York Times*, September 25, 2003, p. C2. (Note that the news did not even make the first business page.)

11. Robert H. Frank and Philip J. Cook, *The Winner-Take-All Society* (New York: Penguin), 1995.

for the winners to make the really big money so often involves illegalities.

Americans, of course, are used to social inequality, and also social mobility. They are taught from childhood that "if you work hard, you can succeed" and that "everyone is entitled to one (or more) mistakes." Positive thinking was invented by and for the Americans, with the "Go West!" option always promising a new start. More than that, the Americans' endowment of natural resources and a vast land taught them early on that one's success was not necessarily because of someone else's failure—"There is enough for everyone." There is no need to be envious of another's success—"You can do it, too."

Globalization would be a cinch if only this mindset was more applicable to the rest of the world. But it is not. In most other societies, particularly those older than America (which includes just about all countries except possibly Canada, Australia, and New Zealand), economic and social progress is much more of a zero-sum game, an "I win/you lose" perception at odds with economic theory but rooted in human nature and past social inequities. This means success is likely to spawn envy and criticism, making the threat of falling behind a more effective motivator than the promise of success. It is important to recognize that in most non-American countries, the individualistic focus and ways of dealing with risks and opportunities are simply not part of the education, the culture, or the social fabric. And of course, neither is the reliance on psychiatrists and lawyers required for the unfettered pursuit of individual gains and losses. The American Way is not for everyone, not even all Americans.

The fact that the gains are uneven would seem still to be a minor issue; after all, everybody is better off than before. But, this is of little or no comfort for the typical individual. As we know from psychology, for most people, the aspirations and expectations that determine their level of satisfaction and happiness are set in comparison with peers, neighbors, and colleagues—the infamous "keeping up with the Jones's" notion. Getting an option of 10 more dollars while your neighbor gets $100, most people will choose none for both. If you don't believe it, try $100 for you and $1000 for your neighbor.[12] If the economic gains are distributed seemingly arbitrarily or by luck and past connections, the envy generated can threaten the social order, as people in the new Russia found out, for example. In that context, it is easy to see why globalization gains are not always welcome. And when it seems the winner does take all, the situation of course gets even worse. You might remember the old "chimpanzees and bananas" jungle experiment, where a previously content and peaceful community of chimpanzees was torn apart by the sudden introduction of a large supply of bananas, quickly hoarded by the strongest male in the flock. The winner-take-all society is more primitive than civilized.

Marketing's Role

In the race to the bottom, marketing has, not unwittingly, played a major role. The freedom accorded to individuals, and the democratic notion of one person–one vote, has meant that it is the majority of the people who decides the direction. Considering the multiracial, multi-ethnic, and multicultural mix of people inhabiting the U.S., the popular choice of a majority naturally involves a "lowest common denominator." Why "lowest?" Because the most advanced and sophisticated expressions or products of a particular race, ethnicity, or culture necessarily require more in-depth appreciation and knowledge of the particular group.

To appeal to a multicultural and multi-ethnic mass market, simple statements about simple things that all can agree on are needed. In politics, in business, and in marketing, messages are kept brief and to the point, especially if the audience is not quite fluent in the language—remember the U.S. data on illiteracy.

----

12. This proposition against "economic man" has been shown to hold in more formal experiments. See *The Economist*, August 9, 2003, p. 62. Economists eager to preserve their self-esteem claim that the results are as expected. If the subjects assume the size of the economic "pie" available is fixed, the only amount that matters is the relative share for each individual.

Lofty appeals intended to inspire virtuous thoughts and behavior are reduced to simple appeals: "Be all you can be." In the commercial marketplace, things are worse. The intense competition combined with the proliferation of products and media lead to the noisy and intrusive in-your-face slogans discussed in this book. Because of the need to be heard over the din in the consumerspace, the promotional sound bytes are louder, more abrasive, and more pervasive. Louder voices dominate softer voices, more shocking images attract more attention, and using more media allows greater reach and frequency. In-your-face marketing complements the product, targeted toward the common denominator for old and new Americans: Convenience and low price, in many ways, are the *only* common denominators for a diverse society.

The need for marketers to appeal to a profitably large group of diverse people easily leads to a dumbing down of commercial messages. This charge has been made about TV and film entertainment, about news media, and about advertising. To make something memorable that sells well among all the disparate subcultures in the U.S. in a certain age group, appeals need to be simple and basic enough to be attractive to millions. Movies, music, and shows, in particular, succumb to this temptation with their sequels and repetitive licks and mantras. They all try to pass "the 7th-grade test." If a 12-year-old can understand it, then it should sell. Market research is also to blame, being focused on the immediate reaction to slogans and visuals rather than on more mature assessments of the appeals. Less in-your-face advertisements are pulled in favor of more graphic visuals and attention-catching action when market researchers use the adrenalin levels, sweaty palms, and dilated pupils of test subjects to choose between commercials.

In many ways, this argument is based on a sense of taste. Yes, the marketing rhetoric is noisy and simple and in your face—but that's perhaps simply the way it seems to me. It's against my "taste." To others, especially the young ones in the target market, the same messages might seem exciting, fun, irreverent, and on the mark. I grant you that. But just remember that, as this book points out repeatedly, even the target audience might not appreciate the volume and noise if it is not in the market, but busy with something else. In addition, you might be exposed to these messages without wanting to be—remember captive marketing! The media options available to the advertisers are so many and so effective (and quite possibly mistargeted) that you might not be able to get away. Even one-to-one marketing might reach you at the most inopportune moments.

When one tries to forge many disparate groups together—the melting pot or new multiculturalism—the result is likely to be a kind of imperfect society. It will not be so cohesive, just like the America we have. The only common symbol we seem to have is the Stars and Stripes. As for shared experiences, well, Americans have shopping and consumption. The spillover into the public arena is predictable: Even the most worthwhile and virtuous causes need advertising and marketing to get noticed. Yes, Americans give a lot—especially after being subjected to the sales pitches of professional fundraisers. The most critical job requirement for a university dean in the U.S. today is typically fundraising capability.[13] You need money to be free and virtuous.

America Is Not the World

My conclusion of these misgivings is that what has been good for America is not necessarily good for the world. Not only is the American society itself suffering from a number of problems, but American democracy and the free market system, under evolution from the founding fathers onward, have meant that the people of the U.S. have been brought up on the individualism dogma and have been trained in individual decision-making. Many foreign countries do not have the same history.

As we have seen, in many ways, the American way of life is a young person's way. Not only is America a young country, its pio-

---

13. Harvard's former president has made an eloquent plea for less commercialization of higher education. See Derek Bok, *Universities in the Marketplace* (Princeton, NJ: Princeton University Press), 2003.

neer culture has morphed into a culture that favors energy over experience, effort over smarts, and excitement over reflection. Few of its elderly and wise citizens seem as relevant as they do elsewhere, especially since the mandate passed on from the old to the young is to change the world for the better, not to find your way in it. True Americans are leaders, not team players. In America, exhortations such as "You can change the world" encourage young people with no trace of irony or cynicism. Apparently most young and impressionable citizens take these sentiments to heart and pass them on to future generations. Marketers follow suit, emphasizing the positive, energetic, and "can-do" attitudes of the young, in the process reinforcing the messages from family and school. This is of course also why Americans have been particularly successful at developing global brands aimed at the younger segments of the population. As this book has stressed, while old-world Europe has developed global brands in luxury products (France, Italy) and traditional industries (Germany, UK, northern Europe), the globally strongest American brands seem particularly suited to the youth markets. Nike, McDonald's, Coca-Cola, and Starbucks tend to target younger, more malleable, and excitable segments, and what they sell are an attitude and a lifestyle.

For many non-Americans, the price they pay for opening their markets is higher than it might seem to Americans. They are not always as prepared for the free market system as the Americans are. The benefits they get are not as great as for the Americans, since many of the products are not customized to their specific culture or environment the way imports here are adapted for Americans. And one should not be surprised to see that many people in other countries look askance at the American way of life. As always, Americans are easily confused about this, since they see so many people yearning for an American immigration green card. They see that there are millions of very poor and oppressed people in the world, and that America offers them the possibility of entry and an opportunity for advancement like no other country. But these are mainly third-world immigrants. There are scores of other people in the world who are doing quite well on their own, thank you, and who don't see the American way as a solution. They resent the need to suffer to make room for the American marketers who seem only interested in making a buck and who use their government to help keep markets open. Even if the economic statistics suggest their folly, these people are ready to put a stop to more products and services from America. They are not necessarily anti-globalization, but they are anti-American.

9 ARE FOREIGN COUNTRIES ANY BETTER?

Where is the grass greener?

Are there preferable alternatives to the commercialized American society? It depends of course on what you want. But sometimes, the news makes you think. For example, the other day I read in the paper about an immigrant family from Ghana who sent two teenage daughters back to Ghana for high school. The idea was for the daughters to get back to their roots, and also to protect them from the lack of discipline and high levels of independence and materialism found in American high schools. Apparently, hanging out with friends had become more important than studying, and their classmates were "just focused on what party to go to." In the Akosombo International School, a boarding school in Ghana, the two sisters encountered a much stricter regiment—dormitory and classroom inspections, early morning jogs on Saturdays, rigidly enforced study and recreation times—which relieved them of the pressure of having too many choices. The sisters' initial apprehension had given way to elation—they couldn't wait to get back to school after spending the summer at home in America.[1]

Another time I heard a review on the radio of a new movie *Thirteen, which begins with the protagonists, two teenage girls, hit-*

---

1. Lynette Clemetson, "For Schooling, A Reverse Emigration to Africa," *The New York Times*, September 4, 2003, pp. A1, A17.

ting each other with fists after taking painkillers, just to find out how insensitive to hurt they have become. According to the reviewer, the movie then proceeded to describe the gradual descent from childhood innocence into casual sex and drugs, the kind of progress that the father from Ghana had been worried about. The film apparently did not end happily—did Hollywood sleep? —but instead, according to the radio reviewer, it offered no solution, no easy out, no comfort for a parent. I was sure I did not want to go see it. The girls stayed lost in the lonely morass of empty materialism and lost innocence, their lives without value and direction. "Just as in real life," the reviewer intoned plaintively to cap off the review, making a point less about the movie than about American society.

I thought of my two daughters. Over the years, we have had several chances go back to Sweden, but I always gave in to their pleas to stay in America. Was this a mistake? I myself was not so sure whether I wanted to go; after all, America seemed meant for young ones like my children. They're happy here, I think, as they should be, since as far as I can judge, American society is designed entirely for their well-being—at least the kind of well-being that comes with extreme consumerism. But maybe they are suffering from all the material choices and dealing with conformity (what brands are cool?) and group norms (how to stand out and belong at the same time?) and the sex and drugs in American high schools? Maybe they would be better off back in old Europe?

My daughters professed in unison their happiness about living in America, but I looked for less biased reassurance. It was not so easy to find. My assistant from the Philippines was back after a month at home to get a permanent work visa for the U.S., and was happy to be back here. But then I read in the paper—I've got to stop reading the news!—that some Chinese professionals had gone back home rather than staying in the U.S. to work. I couldn't help thinking that we can't even get the third world's poor to stay here.

Most Commercialized?

Is the grass greener in other places? Possibly. Even if globalization has so far meant the spread of American commercialism into new countries, this does not mean all countries are now Americanized. There are still plenty of differences among countries. Some of the comparative statistics presented in the previous chapter suggest that there are areas where foreign countries do better. Of course, "better" is a value judgment, and this is not the place to go to great lengths about the various pros and cons of the societies in Europe and Japan, together with Canada and Australia the most obvious alternatives to America. It would take its own book and more. But I can identify those differences that are most relevant to what this book is about: whether there are worthwhile alternatives to the commercialized American way of life, and what role marketing, or the lack of marketing, has played in this.

Focusing on the countries that are responsible for most of the global businesses discussed in this book, an obvious question to ask first is which of the three areas—the U.S., Europe, or Japan—has the most commercialized society? Given all the arguments in this book, the obvious answer should be the U.S. And I think this is the correct answer, although I would make what you might think is a weak qualification. The U.S. has the most obviously commercialized society. It is precisely the obviousness—the "in your face-ness" —of American commercialism that this book deplores and blames on American marketers. It seems a weak qualification because commercialism in many ways seems inherently brash and in your face. But this is not really the case.

The Japanese way

To me—and I suspect for many people who have spent some time in all three contending areas—the most commercialized society by far is Japan. If this seems surprising to some, the reason is probably that in Japan, commercialism has reached a very rarefied and dignified level of artistry. Commercialism in Japan is not brash and in your face at all; it approaches art in its distinguished and refined application. Your first thought should be of the geishas in Kyoto, in their silk kimonos and coiffed hair, playing instruments, conversing or otherwise entertaining well-paying guests. Or you might recall the famous wood-prints by Hokusai of Mt. Fuji, or Hiroshige's Tokaido landscapes, or Utamaro's courtesans, many prints intended as outdoor advertising for eating and lodging establishments. You might also know about the extensive and elaborate gift-giving rituals, cementing goodwill and good business relationships with present and future clients. The Japanese invented relationship marketing in the Edo period, more than 200 years ago.

This is not the place for a complete discussion of what has driven these developments. But I think one factor bears directly on our topic here: Japan has very few natural resources, and has had to trade with foreign countries to obtain needed raw materials. Trading rights were severely curtailed and allotted to only a few trading houses: the sogo shoshas of Mitsubishi, Mitsui, Marubeni, and a few others. To be a trader meant being in the money—marketing, if you want, became a favored business. At the same time, artists were especially valued when providing merchandise, since few natural resources could be marshaled. As my Japanese colleagues like to say, the only natural resource in Japan is people. They are very good at working in teams, helping and supporting one another. They are also aghast at the fact that when they ask me to help get their children into Georgetown, I try but often fail—the fact that they are my friends automatically weakens my voice in the admissions committee. In Japan, it would strengthen the case.

With only slight exaggeration, I would say that in Japan, everybody is a basic economic asset. If people are the only resource, it is not so strange to find that essential decisions in an individual's life have strong commercial elements. You had better leverage your assets, as we say in business school. Take marriage, for instance. Even with the coming of "love matches," a majority of marriages are still arranged, with implicit contracts about duties and obligations, not only for the bride and groom, but also for relatives. Take work as another example. Even though lifetime employment is no longer economically feasible, the company you work for determines not only your salary, but also your status in society, your marriage potential, and your children's prospects. Now consider education. Private universities run high-priced kindergartens with the promise of admissions throughout successive school years. Teachers who grade the severe entrance exams into the prestigious universities might make money by recommending certain cram schools that help to prepare for the questions that will be asked.

Since relationships are so fundamentally commercial, there is little need to stress the point that there is a quid-pro-quo—in fact, it is in bad taste if you do. The Japanese invented the term "honne" to describe the true meaning of what is being said, and "tatemae" for what is actually being stated. The parties in a relationship are supposed to divine honne—the true meaning—from the context of the conversation. Although arranged marriages involve "contracts," these are never explicit and certainly not written down. Obligations to companies and relatives are based on common understanding and unwritten rules. When professors hint that taking a prep course could help your prospects, the hint is just mentioned in passing. This is the notorious "gray area" of Japanese speech that can be so baffling to outsiders—actually, it can be unclear to the Japanese themselves. No wonder there are only a few Japanese lawyers. There might be a need for them because of possible illegalities, but there is no paper trail for lawyers to put their hands on.

This is one reason why the commercialized Japanese society is not brash and in your face. This tradition of indirectness has spilled over into business relationships as well. There is little transparency in Japanese relationships. Business propositions in Japan are never "win-win" or "good for you, good for me"—even advertising is indirect, whimsical, and *not* to the point. The very idea of "marketing" is disdained. Most companies still avoid the idea of having a separate marketing department. "We all do marketing" is a common defense when pressed, and not far from the truth, given their centuries-old honing of commercial relationships.

The European picture

If the Japanese are the most subtle marketers and the Americans are the brashest, the Europeans seem not to take marketing seriously at all. Europe is also, by the same token, the least commercialized area. Europe is of course by no means homogeneous, but in this comparison, it is useful to treat the EU as one and group the countries together.

In northern Europe especially, the tradition in economic life has always been to place production over trading. Endowed with natural resources, the wealth of countries in Europe has always been associated with ownership of land and physical assets. The emphasis was on the extracting of raw materials and manufacturing of products, less with the distribution and selling of the output. Production, not marketing, attracted the most talented people. Even today, a typical promotional appeal of a European brand such as Germany's Beck's beer or the Swedish-made Volvo car is that they are so inept at marketing, not an empty claim.

As in the case of Japan, this is not the place to trace how this development came to pass. Nevertheless, it is useful to highlight one factor. The feudal system, with one landowner employing a number of workers to help exploit the natural resources, was ferociously hierarchical, placing landed gentry at the top. Self-sufficiency was a strong ambition, often necessitating wars to enlarge land holdings and enhance prestige. Trade was a poor alternative when wars failed to deliver the desired possessions, and traders were not well-respected. Having to hawk your wares was embarrassing and was delegated to outsiders and those less fortunate—including the Jewish minorities, generally closed out of property ownership. Still today, many European companies are family-owned or family-dominated, and are run by engineers who came up through manufacturing. They tend to be bad at marketing for these very reasons. They are too sentimental and proud of their products, not able to step back and coolly assess how customers might react. But, they are neither very brash nor in your face; they are more likely to bore customers than to excite them.

I know these generalizations seem a bit like caricatures, and there are certainly exceptions, especially among European companies facing Japanese competition. But when trying to assess whether other countries are any better, these broad outlines are useful for contrasts. For example, take the way the Japanese and the Europeans approach product design. Naturally, the Japanese products in consumer durables are designed and manufactured by engineers, just like the European products are. But, the Japanese engineers, without the baggage of a heritage of natural resources, are concerned not only about building a good product (as are the Europeans), but also about fitting it to people's needs. They call this "Human maximum, machine minimum," emphasizing that people are more important than the product (remember their most valuable asset?). This is how they designed CD players that can be turned off by simply flicking the power off, with no damage to internal circuits, whereas Europeans tell you to first turn off the disk, then the power. Or when Sony realized that Walkman units were easily dropped, the Japanese didn't just warn buyers, but they made sturdier units. The Japanese way is to adapt the products to people, something the Europeans are less wont to do.

If the Japanese are so subtle about their marketing, wouldn't they be upset about the in-your-face approach of the Americans? There is a simple explanation for this: The Japanese cultural and linguistic difference with the West made it necessary to employ natives in the marketing of American products in Japan, and they helped adapt the effort to the Japanese style of subtle and indirect marketing. In Europe, by contrast, the traditional lack of attention to the marketing function opened up a window for a more aggressive American-style effort as post-war Europe rose again with the help of the American Marshall Plan. As we have seen, the legitimacy of this "challenge" was already questioned by the French writer J.J. Servan-Schreiber in 1969.

Some traces of the less commercialized European society can actually be seen in the American South. For pretty much the same reason—a land-owning gentry—the South has maintained a certain aura of a more dignified and peaceful life. For many observers, it is reminiscent of old Europe. But for most practical purposes, the U.S. is really very commercialized and very open about it. If something is for sale, you'll know about it. And even if arranged marriages are not yet in vogue, one day they might well be. What isn't for sale in today's America?

The Vacation Paradox

One effect—actually one sign, if you will—of a thoroughly commercialized society is that everything and everybody has a price. This means that one can use buying and selling transaction explanations for a variety of different phenomena in society. Gary Becker, the 1992 Nobel prize winner in economics from the University of Chicago, has in fact made a career of using supply and demand economics to explain racial discrimination, marriage partners, and how large a family one has.[2] It can also be used to explain why the affluent Americans have such short vacations compared with the "lazy" Europeans.

One of the more revealing statistics about European society is the amount of vacation its workers get. French and German workers routinely collect from 4 to 6 weeks of paid leisure time every year. Since most of the vacation is taken in the summer (when you have six weeks, you might of course save two weeks for a winter resort, if for no other reason than the fact that six weeks on the beach can get pretty boring), the local states making up the German Bundesrepublik stagger vacation times in July and August to make sure the Autobahn does not get completely blocked up with vacation travelers. In Sweden, the father (or better, the mother) of the welfare system, you might even start a new job with a vacation, although no more than four weeks—with some longevity, however, you are soon up to the usual six weeks. The laziness seems to pay off; hourly worker productivity tends to go up with longer vacations. Figures show that productivity for German, French, and Dutch employees is higher than their American counterparts.

The Japanese take very short vacations, typically no more than 4–5 days. And, like Americans, they work long hours, including overtime. Actually, the Americans may get the worst of it all. They work hard and take short vacations, typically about 14 days. According to available data, they even substitute extra work

---

2.   Gary S. Becker, *The Economic Approach to Human Behavior* (Chicago: The University of Chicago Press), 1978.

for the paid leisure time they have earned—many have two jobs.
The work ethic is strong in many of the high-status companies.
Microsoft's top team of Bill Gates and Steve Ballmer used to set a
pace with reportedly 16-hour days, apparently common in high-
tech companies. Even relatively lowly employees get caught—
Wal-Mart associates are sometime pressured into offering free
overtime work.[3]

The busy Americans

Why do the Americans work so hard and take such short vacations? After all, barring temporary slips due to changing
exchange rates, on a per-capita basis, they are the most affluent
people in the world. The typical explanation is the uncertainty
associated with the job situation. As the jobless "recovery" pro-
ceeds, many people feel worried about leaving their current position for any extended period, lest they be fired. This uncertainty
induces people not to stray too far away from their workplace.
This is also one explanation for the Japanese pattern, the loyalty
to the company questioned when staying away longer than a
week. One Japanese salaried worker returned from an overseas
vacation only to find his desk moved out. Who can relax on the
beach when your job might be jeopardized?

An alternative explanation, favored by economists, is that the
opportunity cost of vacations in the U.S. is higher than that in
Europe. Simply speaking, the work alternative in the U.S. brings in
more money than it does in Europe. With less progressive taxes,
they can also keep more of it. A problem with this explanation is
that it seems like Americans, who are already the richest, keep
working simply to make more money. Are there no limits? It surely
looks that way. In other words, it's the "Affluenza" sickness again.
The money is needed for the ever-increasing material needs,
wants, and desires of the American household. Apparently, the
abundance and desire of the people for more and more consumption is what fuels the need for ever more money—and less vacation
time. In a most telling figure, it seems that vacation time is getting

3.   Steven Greenhouse, "U.S. Jury Cites Unpaid Work at Wal-Mart," *The New York Times*, December 20, 2002, p. 26.

shorter as the riches accumulate. There is a negative relationship between income and vacation time.[4] Yes, the opportunity loss of a vacation is great. A longer vacation means that the family has to forego the new SUV. Are two weeks on the beach worth it? Hardly!

A spending vacation

If Europeans take it easy while Americans make money, why is it that the per-day cost of an American family's vacation is higher than that of a corresponding European family's? If the data are to be believed, Americans are bigger spenders than Europeans. Americans are welcome tourists because they tend to spend more than the average visitor—one reason why their absence in Europe after the Iraq war was all the more painful for the continent's businesses. With a short vacation, time is of the essence, especially if opportunity costs are high. To make the time spent seem more valuable, one would want to do more things, see more things, cram more things into the schedule. It becomes more important to stay close to major attractions, to travel faster, to organize the tour more efficiently. This costs money. It might be money well-spent, in the sense that Americans might be able to do many of the things Europeans do on vacations but in half the time. American vacationers are more productive.

These reasons also apply to the Japanese, who traditionally take vacations even shorter than the Americans. The "official" vacation length is typically 14 days, but most people take only 4–5 days, plus a weekend.[5] This brevity is surprising, not only because of the high per-capita incomes of the Japanese, but also because they have far to travel when they go abroad, as many do. It is amazing to learn that they do take 7-day trips to Europe and

---

4.   *The Economist*, August 9, 2003, p. 45. The tradeoff of work for leisure has a long history in economics, and is an area where the "dismal science" doubly deserves its name.

5.   While vacation time was gradually increased to 14 days during the boom in the 1980s, the recession since the early 1990s has undoubtedly helped the Japanese continue their tradition of only 4–5 days away from the office. Johny K. Johansson and Ikujiro Nonaka, *Relentless: The Japanese Way of Marketing* (New York: HarperBuisness), 1996, pp. 11–13.

America, considering it takes almost a full day to get there and another day to go back.

They make up for the short time by preparing carefully, following a tight itinerary produced by a travel agency, and concentrating on main sites only. Japanese tourist groups with their cameras are of course a very familiar sight to most people—they take their pictures outside the monuments, they buy souvenirs, and then they move on. And, of course, they spend money to get gifts for people back home. As some of my Japanese friends say, their vacation trips tend to consist of three stages: *before* (which entails a lot of work), *during* (a very tiring stage), and *after* (which is the only truly enjoyable part, when stories and memories can be aired and elaborated freely over beer and sake).

Which leads us all the way back to the question of why have a vacation in the first place. If it is so much work, why bother? And here is perhaps the most telling glimpse of the differences between countries in terms of lifestyles, quality of life, and standard of living: Vacations in the consumerspace of the Americans tend to be a matter of spending money for goods and services, the definition of having a good time, while European vacations are a time to slow down and get out of the usual rut of consumerism.

A Day in the Life

How people live in different societies varies not only by per-capita income and demographics. The way of life differs greatly because of history and cultural traditions. These are the things that create all these differences we hear about in Europe. The French like cheese and the British are beefeaters. The Germans prefer sausages and beer, while the Italians love spaghetti. In terms of socio-economics the differences may not be that great, and even though you can get pasta and wine anywhere, unique local cultures are still to be found inside most of these countries. The EU integration, just like globalization, has tended to energize and strengthen domestic cultures, at the same time adapting them to the presence of new foreign elements. Perhaps the most striking example of this is the way American culture has simply been added to traditional Japanese customs. In Tokyo's Ginza, you can see kimono-clad women on the street eating ice cream and drinking Coca-Cola, or spot a man in Harajuku's weekend throng whom you recognize as the formal businessman you met at a company last Monday—only now he is on a motorcycle in Levi's jeans and biker boots.

When we marketers group countries according to various cultural and way-of-life indicators, we very often find that America is different from all the others—an *outlier*, in statistical language. The prime reason for this is the diversity of the American population; sometimes, you might even be tempted to say that there really isn't any one "American culture." We have touched on this before and the way that the diversity can lead to a lack of shared values and experiences and a resulting least common denominator approach to promotional messages. The more homogeneous cultures of other countries allow more complexity in the messages, a deeper understanding of people, and a greater role for non-verbal communication and subtle nuances in speech. At the same time, as we say in global marketing, these "high-context" cultures are difficult to transfer across countries, while the "low-context" American way, which makes sure that everything that needs to be said gets said, travels well. With only slight exaggeration, in the low-context American culture, if you didn't say it, you didn't mean it—and what you said is what you meant. But of course, this seems awfully crude to many people from high-context cultures who long for that implicit understanding that needs no words.

The diversity in America hinders the imposition of common constraints. There is not much "common" in common sense. Compared to other countries, social norms are weak, and the motivation to comply is lacking. When rules are actually imposed, the diversity makes enforcement weak. It naturally leads to a "pluralistic" tradition, allowing for more variability when public officials interpret regulations. It also leaves a vacuum that media advertising and marketing efforts can fill. Americans learn how to act and talk from television, and their heroes are celebrities that make most of their money as spokespersons for products and services.

But, this looseness in enforcement also means greater flexibility. In more homogeneous societies, stricter rules and regulations can be enforced because of commonly accepted standards. It makes for orderly societies, but also makes it difficult for the culture to accommodate new immigrants, outsiders, and deviants. In America, an immigrant can feel welcome and at home within a few months. In a homogeneous culture with more unwritten rules, the immigrant will always feel—and be treated as—an outsider.

Patriotism

A good example of how in-your-face marketing efforts have infected society is the way Americans display their patriotism. Even before the war on terrorism, Americans would wear their patriotism "on their sleeve," as it were, brazenly exhibiting the flag the way winning athletes now run victory laps. Wrapping oneself in the colors of the flag also makes the in-your-face expressions of championship—"We're number 1"—more telegenic, and you can easily get the impression that American patriotism is made for TV. Now, of course, other countries' athletes do the same, but usually without the flair and finger-pointing that Americans excel at. When it comes to being in your face, Americans are still the champs. As Arnold Schwarzenegger replied when defending Madonna's open-mouth kiss of Britney Spears at the MTV video music awards: "When they decide the one shot from the whole show that's going to be in *The LA Times* or *The New York Times*, is it going to be you, or is it going to be someone else? I can relate to that."[6]

Patriotic expressions in other countries tend to be more ambivalent, mainly tainted by a history of warring with neighboring nations, a tradition that is not always heroic and dignified. Also, since the more homogeneous cultures tend to have many more layers of shared experiences than the diverse Americans, there is less need to focus on overt expressions of patriotism. You don't feel comfortable stating the fact that you love your nation—and, as always, if you feel the need to be explicit about it, others might

---

6. As quoted by Maureen Dowd, *The New York Times*, September 25, 2003, p. A27.

doubt your sincerity. What it comes down to, again, is that many foreign people will view Americans as having bad taste. Americans, of course, don't care; they are used to thinking that "my taste is as good as any."

But what about France? Isn't France more chauvinistic—it's their word for one thing—than other countries? For example, the French government has ruled out the use of anglicized words in the language, using "ordinateur" for computer and "courriel" for e-mail, and it requires that 40% of all radio playlists be French songs. France is also the country most intent on making itself and the EU the political and military counterweight to any American hegemonic power. Isn't this in-your-face patriotism?

Here, Alexis de Tocqueville, the French author of the famous 1834 travel report "Democracy in America," will be of some use. His take on American patriotism is that it is personalized, that it ascribes to the nation the same characteristics you ascribe to a person.[7] By contrast, in France, patriotism involves a celebration of something greater than the individual citizen, with traits beyond the purely personal. This helps explain the ease with which Americans take to the flag, and the awkwardness of many other people using the flag for personal aggrandizement. It also helps explain the fact that on Bastille Day, the French can parade their military forces down the Champs Elysees with obvious pride, while American Independence Day is a day for family picnics. American expressions of patriotism might be in your face, but they are rarely a show of force, except, that is, until the new unilateralism.

The marketing of religion

Religion in America presents another striking example of in-your-face commercialization. The insistent marketing efforts by churches and preachers in the U.S. to attract converts stand in stark contrast to the more traditional European pattern. In the U.S., enterprising preachers have translated missionary zeal into salesmanship, developed products and promotional programs,

---

7. Alexis de Tocqueville, *Democracy in America*, Vol.2, Third Book (New York: Vintage Books), 1945 reprint.

growing the number of contributing customers to their churches by intensive marketing efforts. Thus, you can find TV stations run by churches, TV programs syndicated across the country—so that the preacher can reach beyond the local market—and even a university founded by a preacher who named it for himself, The Bob Jones University (of course, my own Georgetown University was founded by a Jesuit priest). Successful preachers like Billy Graham and Jerry Falwell, much like Bill Gates at Microsoft and Steve Jobs at Apple, have become media celebrities, and one, Pat Robertson, was even mentioned as a potential presidential candidate at one point.

Religion plays a major role in the daily life of the American people. If one is to believe statistics, church attendance in America is far above that of Europeans. As many as 30% of all Americans claim to go to church at least once a week. The corresponding figure for many Europeans is below 5%. Even in a country such as Italy, where regular churchgoing is more common, not many in the congregation stay around to meet the priest after the service the way they commonly do in the U.S. Given the churchgoing crowds in America, it is not surprising that the number of marketing activities has steadily increased. After all, this can be a large market for the right products and services. And the constitutional separation of religion and state in America has privatized a market which elsewhere is strictly regulated.

There can be little doubt that religious questions in secular Europe have played themselves out. The religious wars have settled matters. After the Thirty-Year War ended in 1648 in Westphalia, the Protestants essentially populated northern Europe, and Wallenstein and his Catholic army preserved the south for the Pope. Henry VIII had already established a Church of England independent of Rome. With the one big exception of the Jewish question, the later wars in Europe—the Napoleonic wars, the 1870–71 German-French conflict in Alsace-Lorraine, the big conflagrations in the 20th Century, and others—had no religious overtones. This is very different from countries elsewhere, such as the Middle East. Religion has not stirred nationalistic emotions in Europe for a long time.

Historical reasons surely also help explain why Americans go to church. The early arrivals to the New World were the dissenting religious groups that had suffered in the European religious wars: the Puritans from England, the Huguenots from France, the Calvinists from central Europe, and so on. Anybody with some pride in his or her heritage would like to pay homage to past generations, and staying true to the original quest by going to the church of one's choice is a small price to pay. This contrasts sharply with Europe, since not only is religion associated with devastating wars, but churchgoing obligations are not to family and predecessors, but to the King or the distant Pope. In Europe, it is harder to believe that God is just and supports you.

The Japanese story is again entirely different, with its history of Buddhism and Shintoism. Briefly, the secularity of Japanese society comes from a long history of using religion for various functional and economic purposes. In Shintoism, the Emperor is the head of the shrine, which is mainly used for ceremonial purposes (as in the controversial annual visits by the Prime Minister to the Yasukuni shrine housing war-time dead). For a price, blessings can be provided for assuring a successful and prosperous business. Buddhism and its temples and monks are also incorporated closely with economic and political activities, with carefully orchestrated events like marriages and funerals.[8] Many Japanese seem cynical about religion, but also pleased that Christianity has been held at bay for three centuries or more.

Recalling the American stress on excitement, energy, and youth, one might wonder whether better marketing would help revitalize religion in Europe again. Is it possible that through more intensive "product development" and "promotional" efforts, people in Europe could be energized and motivated to go to church, to make religion more important in their lives, to nurse a European Billy Graham? I hardly think so, but I have been wrong before. It

---

8. By contrast, religion plays a small role for individual behavior, social norms being all-important. As a leading Japanese social anthropologist asserts: "The Japanese have no religious practice or belief that controls individual thinking and behavior." Chie Nakane, *Japanese Society* (Tokyo: Charles E. Tuttle), 1970, p. 155.

is very difficult to believe that the ironic, cynical, detached, and sophisticated—and old—Europeans could dispel their doubts and muster up the youthful enthusiasm necessary for true faith. But then, the television shows of Oprah Winfrey and Dr. Phil are already very successful in Europe, and they may be the foot-in-the-door that the church needs. Can Jerry Falwell be far behind?

Your Choice

In the end, yes, the grass might be greener elsewhere. Even with open markets and globalization, there are differences between countries, in their degree of commercialization, in their work and leisure habits, in their way of life. You can still get away from in-your-face marketing efforts and escape the consumerspace. You can decide that what you want is more structure and discipline for your children without the temptations of the mall and the television. You can find places on the earth where reflection and reasoning beat energy and action, only they won't be in America.

But going there, whether it is to Europe, Japan, or elsewhere, you do give up some of the American dynamism and vitality, no question. If your druthers are to stay young forever, America is the better place. But as you grow older, it gets harder and harder to keep that up. America re-invents itself constantly, making for frustration among people who thought they were with it, but "it" changed (as *The Simpsons'* grampa puts it). I remember giving a speech at Tokyo's giant ad agency Dentsu in the early 1990s, pointing to the recent election of President Clinton as evidence of how an economically weak and scorned America could quickly shift gears. The Japanese had their own troubles—the financial bubble had burst and the Nikkei stock-market index was sinking—and I said I hoped the equally recent marriage of the Crown Prince to Masako-san might mean a similar rebound for Japan. I was wrong. The Japanese have lost a decade and more, preferring the status quo and social cohesion to new initiatives and painful change. No pain, no gain.

10 ACCENTUATE THE POSITIVE

It could be worse.

How *far have we come? Is marketing absolved of sin or is it still tainted? Is anti-globalization justified or just a knee-jerk reaction by traditionalists? Is anti-Americanism just an expression of envy of the sole superpower?*

The answers I come up with are not encouraging, but I will try to "accentuate the positive and eliminate the negative," as Bing Crosby and the Andrews Sisters suggested at another tense time in international relations, early 1945. Let's first look at what can be concluded about the three strikes and then I would like to offer some advice for global marketers and consumers.

The Pro-Marketing Case

I am least optimistic about the pro-marketing case, especially as it plays out in the U.S. After going through the anti-marketers' concerns about marketing, as we have done here, it would be nice to find that most of the complaints have been taken care of and those that remain are relatively minor. I think that neither is correct.

I would like to say that there are some positive signs, but honestly, I don't see any. Take the Hummer, for example. Even with oil prices soaring, it apparently sells as well as ever, as do the other SUVs. Even the foreign manufacturers have gotten into the sport-utility segment. In fact, most new SUVs sold in America are now made by foreign manufacturers in American plants, resulting in a flooded market and difficulties for Ford and other American automakers. America's love affair with big trucks is being celebrated in the media, one suspects as a way to rekindle patriotism and a return to "true American" makes. The electric car is off the market, leaving a small and tiny—albeit growing—share for the hybrids. No, the automakers and their customers show little sign of common sense or concern for others.

Next consider the Internet marketers and the empowered consumer. We know that the amount of advertising done on the busy Web sites (the banner ads, the pop-ups, the "rich-media" ads, and what have you) has come down. They simply did not work because people did not click on the ads for unwanted products (score one for the sane consumer). But now the Web ads are for more relevant offerings. There are pop-up ads for software that stops pop-ups, banners that hawk virus-protection programs, and ads that greet you personally and think they know your taste because once you bought a present for a distant relative. We also get *spam*, or junk e-mail offers, and e-mail offers about how to stop spam. We get warnings about the most recent computer viruses and worms and what the differences are; we learn how to download programs that explain how to run protection software and we never open unknown attachments. As they say, with the Internet we can do things we couldn't even dream of before.

In the larger picture, producers have been empowered as much or more by the Internet than consumers. Even if the outright selling of customer records from e-commerce transactions has been precluded by privacy laws, clever formulations of accessibility permissions let some firms off the hook. Organizations are cutting back on their telephone operator staff by redirecting you to their Web sites, where you have to do all the heavy lifting—and where "Contact Us" clicks lead you into cyberspace. If you don't pay your bills over the Internet, the bank might levy a surcharge for having to deal with a check. Staying on the phone, you have to press your way through a labyrinth-like option tree to get to customer service—where the person is "busy serving other customers." Many companies even use ingenious software that computes how long you will have to wait—"approximately 12 minutes; please stay on the line; your call will be answered in turn." I remember when we used to teach in the business school that for good service, a company should answer the phone at least by the third ring. In many organizations—including in my school—the technology center has become the most critical resource holding the key, quite literally, to any productive work.

The telemarketing case seemed at one point to be a bright spot, with over 50 million phone numbers registered in the Federal Trade Commission's (FTC's) DoNotCall.com registry. But the legality of the registration continues to be challenged, even after the U.S. Congress intervened with a lopsided vote (95 to 0 in the Senate, 412 to 8 in the House) in favor of the FTC.[1] I am basically against government intervention in economic matters, but since a majority of the American people are set against the continuation of the telemarketing nuisance, couldn't the marketers simply let go? If the products and services sold are worthwhile, surely there are other ways to get them to the attention of potential customers? Even my colleagues at the business school agree with me on this point. Some even argue that telemarketing is not marketing, but pure and simple selling. I agree, but so are many other "marketing" practices.

How about the "fast-food nation" issues? Aren't we doing better with the fat content in hamburgers and with obesity? There has been a lot hand-wringing in the media about the fact that many of the poorer Americans—there are more and more of them if official statistics are to be believed—end up overweight because the cheaper foods they eat are dangerously high in fat. The high sugar content also leads to increased rates of diabetes among children, again according to statistics. I am hopeful that these dire numbers help people adjust, but I am not sure they want to. Fatty and sweet foods are tasty—and cheap—stomach-fillers. McDonald's and other chains have apparently introduced lower fat hamburgers,

---

1. "'Do-not-call' List Faces More Hang-ups," *CNNMoney.com*, September 25, 2003.

chicken meals, and more fresh produce. Do we know who buys and eats those choices? I am not sure. Leaner food does not fill you up the way a Big Mac does. Knowing a little about how we marketers have conditioned people from childhood with sweet and buttery foods (Did you know that baby food is sugary primarily because the mothers like it, helping the baby develop a sweet tooth?), I can't help but think that it will take a long time before poorer people will change their eating habits, especially if it's going to cost money. The last I heard, funeral casket manufacturers have even adjusted to market conditions. The Goliath Casket company of Lynn, Indiana is doing brisk business in oversized coffins.[2]

The selling of monopoly access to students, patients, and employees has reached new heights. Marketing consulting firms have cropped up, helping universities, high schools, hospitals, and other marketing novices negotiate favorable contracts, giving exclusive sales and advertising rights to soft drink firms, food vendors, and pharmaceutical companies. The money involved can be staggeringly large given the typical budget of the organizations involved. When New York City approved a deal with Snapple to let the company be the sole provider of drinks in its vending machines, Snapple paid $166 million for a five-year deal. Experts still argued that the price for the contract was too low given the captive market size. For example, New York's 1,200 public schools will "only" net $8 million a year for the school board. The school board's case was not helped when it was disclosed that Snapple's product line, mainly relatively healthy juices, contained more sugar than the typical cola.[3]

With parents mounting opposition to the encroachment of the soft drink companies into the schools, Coca-Cola announced that the company would roll back all its marketing efforts to children under 12 years of age. In seemingly another win for restraint and decency, the company vowed that there would be no television

---

2.   Warren St. John. "On the Final Journey, One Size Doesn't Fit All," *The New York Times*, September 28, 2003, Sec. 1, p. 1.

3.   Marian Burros, "The Snapple Deal: How Sweet It Is," *The New York Times*, September 17, 2003, pp. D1, D6.

ads, no free coupons, and no giveaways like book covers emblazoned with the company's logo. At the same time, however, consumer groups learned that Coca-Cola Enterprises had become the official sponsor of the National Parents and Teachers Association (PTA) advocacy group that protects the health of children. In addition, a Coca-Cola lobbyist was appointed to the National PTA board, to "help its marketing effort."[4] No wonder some parents feel that Coca-Cola has managed to substitute direct influence on school children for more expensive paid advertising to them.

Finally, brand building continues as the headline mantra of the marketing community. As competitors benchmark each others' new products, true differentiation is impossible to sustain and competition revolves around intangibles, basically brand name and image. As before, to leverage across all the promotional media—traditional broadcast and print, and also the Internet, e-mail, cable TV, and cell phones—companies focus on a few main brands, and try to impress their logos on the collective unconscious. I see no relief in the assault, but rather greater efforts by the companies, more consulting agencies popping up to help with brand-building strategies, and new courses in our business schools. We are now offering six-week elective courses for our MBAs in "How to Build Strong Brands" and "The Marketing of Consumer Goods," in addition to our traditional functional courses on "Product Management," "Pricing," and "Advertising."

The branding emphasis is also part and parcel of a stress on marketing "metrics," one of the highest priorities in the Marketing Science Institute, an industry-supported funding agency for research in marketing. Marketing metrics involve putting hard dollar figures on the "bottom line" of marketing efforts. One example of such metrics is the effort, discussed in Chapter 2, to translate a strong brand name into a brand equity dollar figure. Not surprisingly, such a focus of marketers on hard financials leaves little if any consideration for the empowerment of the consumer or the role of marketing in commercializing our society.

---

4. Sherri Day, "Coke Moves with Caution to Remain in Schools," *The New York Times*, September 3, 2003, pp. C1, C5.

The Pro-Globalization Case

The pro-globalization case gives some reason for optimism. True, the Doha round of WTO-sponsored trade negotiations ended badly in Cancun, Mexico, but the reasons were clear and entirely predictable given the third-world countries' situation and the anti-globalizers' agenda.[5] The fact is that many of the issues demanded by the anti-globalizers have been resolved or are finally getting the attention needed for further progress. If one discounts the more radical and violent anti-globalizers, the movement has had considerable success.

The biggest effect so far might be the cessation and improvement of various sweatshop practices in third-world countries engaged in by outsourcing multinational firms. Although some practices still persist and not all firms have improved equally, the conditions in many countries with respect to child workers, the treatment of women, and environmental degradation are much better because of the anti-globalization movement. The efforts will necessarily have to be persistent, as progress will need to be monitored for continued compliance, but the issues are front-stage and firms know the power of disparagement of these practices. Nike's attempt to gain goodwill for its efforts was thwarted in the courts as "commercial speech," requiring objective verification, but the company still seems to have rebuilt some of its favorable image.[6] The anti-globalizers also claim success and argue that getting the global brand leaders to change means that other manufacturers will follow.

Other positives involve the WTO's successful effort to get drug manufacturers to release their proprietary claims on certain drugs, in particular AIDS medications, and allow some third-world countries to produce generic versions of the drugs. Under pressure from anti-globalizers as well as various economists, the IMF has shown much more flexibility when imposing lending

---

5.   Diego Cevallos, "WTO-Cancun: Future Uncertain After Collapse of Talks," *Inter Press Service*, September 14, 2003.

6.   Stanley Holmes, "Free Speech or False Advertising?" *Business Week*, April 28, 2003, p. 69.

requirements on countries, and the Argentina case seems to be heading toward a reasonable resolution. World Bank President James Wolfensohn has come out strongly against corruption in third-world governments, but he is also in favor of taking local economic, ethnic, and cultural idiosyncrasies into account when designing assistance programs for the poor, a kind of localization thrust at the macro-economic level.[7] By and large, the anti-globalization movement has forced the large international organizations to show greater sensitivity to the demands of the poorer countries.

The same process is also likely to take place when it comes to agricultural subsidies, those government funds that enable farmers in Europe and the U.S. to grow wheat, corn, cotton, and other staples and then dump crops at below-market prices on the world market, undercutting third-world producers. This egregious practice, a flagrant violation of a global free trade regime, was the most immediate cause of the breakdown in Cancun. While a united front of 21 third-world producers demanded a reduction of the subsidies, the Europeans and Americans demanded reciprocal concessions on the part of the poor countries.[8] The arrogance of the developed nations in asking for equal concessions is an example of attitudes that are no longer sustainable in the globalization process. Given their record so far, and the global economic and political realities, anti-globalizers will sooner or later force the rich nations to yield. The rich have to share more of their wealth.

As we have seen, more and more global companies now try to adapt their offerings to local markets. Menus in global fast-food restaurants increasingly differ across countries, giving more autonomy to local managers. At the same time, local specialties with promise elsewhere are introduced abroad for greater variety, just the way globally coordinated marketing is supposed to work. Local brands with loyal followings are rejuvenated, sometimes with the infusion of foreign capital from a global competitor

---

7.   Rich Thomas, "Is Lord Jim That Bad?" *Newsweek*, January 28, 2002, p. 43.

8.   Cevallos, op.cit., 2003.

whose own brand is held back. You may argue that this is still global domination, but at least the capital infusion is not as transient as the portfolio flows on the financial markets.

In more mature economies, the pattern of merging past traditions with the received global consumer culture is even more striking. These countries use globalization to generate new ideas and then combine these ideas in new ways with traditional country skills. As a result, advanced countries are not only recipients of global influences, they also exert influence over other cultures. The ubiquitous Swatch watches from Switzerland, Benetton apparel from Italy, the French Bic pen, and Kung Fu movies from Hong Kong are all part of the globalization process. Popular rock bands and artists come from "wherever"—Kraftwerk from Germany, the Cranberries from Ireland, the Hives from Sweden, Canada's Alanis Morissette. The mobile phone craze has been fanned by designs from Finland's largest company, Nokia. The Japanese, of course, with their focus on fun and fantasy for the free-spending young ones (Pokemon, Hello Kitty), are in many ways as responsible as America for the global consumer culture.

Globalization has not been a one-way street. Even a country such as India, in many ways a late-comer to globalization, has become an "emitter" of global influence, with its software engineering in Bangalore, its huge film industry now reaching most of South Asia and soon to engulf northern countries, and of course, its transcendental gurus whose global networks helped define consumer culture as far back as the 1960s.

The Pro-American Case

I am cautiously optimistic about the anti-American situation. I don't mean that other countries and societies will soon embrace the American way of life and its commercialized culture. Quite the contrary; they will continue to resist any American attempts at economic and cultural domination. But Americans will change. As you have seen, many American corporations have already started to become more sensitive to local differences. This will also happen in the political sphere of international relations, and then the anti-American sentiments will wane. The basic problem is Bush, not America. The repositioning of "Brand America" to a unilateral imperial power has not worked and will not work. America's traditional values of freedom and tolerance of diversity will re-assert themselves both at home and internationally. This is likely to happen whether Bush is at the helm or not, but for him to stay on requires a 180-degree turnaround. The only chance for the present policy to succeed is if a major terrorist attack on the U.S. mainland would again take place.

These are not really very original thoughts anymore, which is why I think the prediction is quite reliable. Most people I meet are basically of the same opinion, regardless of party affiliation. The intensity of their feelings varies, but the basic sentiments are shared: The President's policies (his "product line") have to be modified and improved, and there is even a need for that Detroit standby, a model "recall." I would also predict that he and his staff will see the need for this, and will come clean with the citizens of the U.S. and with our allies abroad. America will cease its America-first unilateralism and embrace the traditional multilateral international role.[9]

It is interesting and intriguing to see how marketing analysis is applied by many observers to explain what is happening to Bush's handling of the Iraq war, the major issue in the anti-Americanism movement. There is still some disagreement on whether the problem is in communications or whether the policy itself (the "product") is faulty. Many people, including myself, think that the problem is in maintaining complete control of Iraq, asking for international help without yielding authority to participating countries or the UN. That is a product problem, not simply a communications issue. It is the same attitude that reflected itself

---

9. I say this even though the administration's actions continue to frustrate. On top of the denial of bidding rights for Iraq contracts to France and Germany and other countries, U.S. plans to contest more stringent U.N. rules to battle global obesity (Rob Stein, "U.S. Says It Will Contest WHO Plan to Fight Obesity," *The Washington Post*, January 16, 2004, p. A3). But especially with the election approaching, public opinion will force a retreat from these in-your-face tactics on the international stage.

in the American unwillingness to yield on agricultural subsidies in the Cancun WTO negotiations.

Others maintain that the basic problem lies primarily with Bush's in-your-face approach to communications. Some marketers argue that there are better ways of telling the Iraq story. One suggestion is that the White House should feature stories and pictures of Iraqi young people whose future is now much brighter than before, a kind of public relations solution to anti-Americanism that seems designed to target readers of *People* magazine and the *Oprah Winfrey* television audience.[10] Coming from marketing experts, this suggestion confirms my pessimistic assessment of the future of marketing in this country, pulling political communications down to the level of deodorants, detergents, and dishwashing liquids.

Meanwhile, the Bush administration is still trying to sell the war using typical hard-sell techniques. His request for $87 billion in support for the Iraq effort, and his appeal to the UN for other countries' participation, continued to feature a positive spin on the justification for the war and America's "success" in the war, with no apologies. It reminded me of the Harvard MBA's semi-official motto: "Often wrong, but never in doubt." The administration's top "salespeople" (now a routine media phrase for the top cabinet members of the Bush administration) were dispatched to present the sales pitch to various television audiences. But from a marketing perspective, the task is becoming similar to trying to sell a defective product. Claims concerning the WMDs and biological warfare were overplayed. The speedy conquest of Baghdad sounds hollow as American soldiers continue to get killed. The safety and security of average people are lower than before. If the marketing history of product recalls is any guide, these are the kinds of issues that need to be honestly acknowledged and apologized for before asking for the support of U.S. citizens and foreign allies.

---

10. Jennifer Wells, "Big Bucks Won't Buy Respect for 'Brand America,'" *Toronto Star,* March 5, 2003, p. A06.

This is why I think these selling efforts will fail to convince Americans and certainly will fail to convince foreign allies. I also think the Bush administration will realize this sooner or later, and will in fact retreat and regroup. One effect from such a regrouping will be a renewed sense of comradeship between America and its allies. Once the U.S. shows a sincere willingness to admit its errors and appeals for assistance on a more equitable basis, allies are more than likely to fall in line. One would also hope that this new attitude would extend itself to the third world and the free trade problems, but for the present version of anti-Americanism, these are not such key issues. Anti-Americanism among Western and other advanced countries is a fruit of an unwillingness to consider them worthy partners, and can be resolved once this attitude is eradicated.

It might be argued that election pressure will force Bush to "stay on message" with upbeat assertions about the Iraq war and continued denigration of former allies, especially the French. But this is really selling the American voters short. The evidence of the mistakes made in and about Iraq is massive and can no longer be ignored with a stiff upper lip. As another American president allegedly said, "You can't fool all the people all the time." This is also why it is likely that we will see much less negative press about Europe in the next few months. As became clear in the course of doing the work for this book, the anti-Americanism attributed to the Europeans in the last few months in the American media has been vastly overplayed, reflective more of an anti-European or anti-French attitude here in the U.S. than a true picture of European sentiments toward the U.S. Given the way the White House has tried to sell its story about the war, a marketer such as myself can easily get the impression that the alleged anti-Americanism is a marketing tactic employed by pro-Bush forces. The solitary leader betrayed by allies plays well in the overall message.

In the end, I am more optimistic than that. This anti-Americanism is a temporary phase. Barring another major terrorist attack in the U.S., this country will revert to its greater ideals and be true to them. Americans will realize that they need others, just as others need them.

Good Global Marketing

Most of the discussion in this book of global marketing practices and the anti-globalization reaction to them has suggested that global marketers have gone too far in foisting their products and brands on the populace as a kind of replacement for traditional culture and religious norms. According to this argument, modern marketing techniques as developed primarily in America are intrusive and inherently disruptive, and the global brand marketers have to share some responsibility for inciting negative reactions.

As we have seen, this argument does not hold up entirely when confronted with the way the various markets have reacted to foreign brand entries. Instead, most open markets, including those in less developed countries, have been able to achieve some accommodation of the global forces. Local traditions and culture have been resurgent, and rather than being dominated by the global brand entries, new hybrid forms and alternatives have been developed. Undoubtedly there have been losses in terms of local businesses, products, and brands, but the globalization process, as promised, seems to have created more dynamism and entrepreneurship among indigenous populations. This finding is particularly striking when contrasted with the relative weakness in Japan's economy, where global influences have been actively resisted.

Nevertheless, anti-globalization activists have a point. Even though the countries might be strong enough to withstand and even profit from the challenge, the market entries from abroad do constitute an invasion, an attack on established brands, loyalties, and ways to do business. While young people might have an easier time adapting to the continually changing marketplace, most people will find some aspects of it to be unsettling and uncomfortable. Warfare does not make for peace of mind.

What does this mean for managerial action in the multinationals? It implies a number of things, not the least of which is that anti-globalization, in particular anti-Americanism, is latent in many foreign countries and can flare up easily. It also means that there are ways in which the American marketer can help prevent fires—or help stoke them, if not careful.

Remember that the free choice offered by marketers in newly opened markets poses problems for many consumers. They may not have the means to buy the products even if they want them, the price being too high for their incomes. Or, they might have been satisfied with the old brands, and the new entrant shakes them out of their comfortable beliefs, like they preferred their old Chrysler. Or, the new brand's main benefits may involve needs that the consumers did not know they had, such as different sneakers for running, cross-training, walking, and aerobics, in addition to those for different sports, needs which are created by marketers.

These negatives of free choice that can create consumer frustration and disillusion with open markets can be overcome. Not only should the marketer stand behind the product fully, warranting its functional and emotional satisfaction, but the marketer needs to take the potential customer's situation into account, presenting products and services that have a clear need to fulfill and are adapted to the consumer's situation. This should not be a questionable proposition for any marketer. It also means that the promotional communications—and promises—accompanying the offer need to be sensitive and framed appropriately for the consumer's situation.

Local adaptation is not simply the best strategy to overcome any latent anti-globalization sentiments, it is the only strategy. Local adaptation is of course helped considerably by the advances in modular design and flexible manufacturing. But with the economies of scale in platform designs, standardized components, operating manuals, and single brand names, there is still a strong degree of uniformity in a company's product and service across different countries. A McDonald's restaurant in Beijing, run by a Chinese franchisee, is still at its core the American hamburger icon—the company makes sure of that. If not up to its (American) standards, the contract will be voided. A Honda built in Ohio is still up to the quality of Hondas from Japan—the company marquee guarantees that. The same is true for all well-run global companies. But now, more needs to be done.

For most managers, the question of global localization is a matter of where to strike the optimal balance between localization and standardization. This calculation needs to consider not only demand factors and cost efficiencies, but potential anti-globalization sentiments as well. Especially with the new marketing techniques, touting relationship-building, experiential marketing, and branding communities, the audience is likely to go beyond the immediate customers. The most visible global marketers are necessarily noticed outside their immediate market segments, and the spillover effect is not obviously positive. The solution is now to strike another kind of balance, between local responsiveness to the society at large and the branding imperative for marketers to always communicate the same message. IMC might seem like an ideal from a marketing perspective, but it is counterproductive when it means a mind-numbing oversell of foreign brands—and potential antipathy from a populace sick of commercialization.

A marketing strategy that avoids stirring anti-globalization fervor needs to have two things. First, a product needs to be localized completely, including changes in the product's design, ingredients, formulation, size and style of packaging, pricing, and so on. Second, promotional communications need to be adapted not only in terms of language and benefit explanations, but also in terms of usage suggestions. The changes involved can be minor for developed countries, but are likely to be major for many developing countries.

Clearly, many of the scale returns involved in going global will be lost with this approach. But this places the critical entry decision precisely where it belongs: Where these adaptations are deemed too costly because economies of scale are lost, the brand should not be introduced. If it is introduced anyway, unchanged and with a standardized promotional campaign emphasizing brand meaning and identity, it not only creates frustration among some people and helps divide the society into haves and have-nots, it also kindles emotional resentment against the foreign elements. This can be a recipe for how to get anti-globalization feelings aroused.

Transcending Consumerism

Finally, some words to the consumers in the U.S.: It is really time to grow up. Hedonism might be all right for teenagers, but it is too shallow for the citizens of a country that thinks itself number one in the world.

I think the solution involves a kind of transcendence, not simply because Emerson and his transcendentalism is American, although that strengthens the advice. To transcend means having a certain discipline over one's emotions, a certain coolness and distance to one's immediate desires. It requires maturity and involves a diminished level of abandon. You may go crazy the first time you get a car, a house, a boat, but later this cools off—you transcend.

In this context, transcendence would mean to recognize that consumption experiences are perfectly acceptable, but they do not constitute an end in themselves. To transcend products and brands means not "getting caught" by them. A life that does not go beyond individual consumption is a poor life, and will only, as is well-documented, be sustainable with ever larger doses of the consumption drug. Aspiration levels keep rising indefinitely.

The idea of transcendence relates directly to today's techniques of brand marketing. Whatever the brand builders want from you, transcendence it is not. They want you to get excited about the brand, attach a special meaning to it (and not to competing brands), and identify and bond with the brand so it becomes more than an accessory: You are the brand. Nothing could be further from cool transcendence. Sure, anyone can get excited about a new Mac notebook, but soon it becomes just a part of your life, not bad, just nice. Then the exaggerated promotions will strike you as absurd, and easily generate a kind of sense of having been taken for a ride.

The reason transcendence is important for brands of products and services is that you generally want to avoid global brands just because they are that, global. As a consumer, you should not be against trying, testing, and even buying global brands—just don't get caught with them as the "ultimate." I have met too many people who proclaimed their absolute allegiance to this or that beer, and then found them a month or so later doing the same for another beer label. There is nothing wrong with this, you just need to realize how naive statements like, "I will never drink an import ale again" or, "You will not find me behind the wheel of a Japanese car" are. Enjoy the variety and proliferation of competing brands, local as well as global—just don't get married to one of them, however much they propose.

No Globalized Uniformity, Please

In the end, globalization's weakest point from a marketing perspective might be that it could succeed too well, homogenizing all the markets of the world. The uniformity would surely make for a very uninteresting planet. If local products and brands are eliminated and the same global products and brands appear everywhere, there is little adventure and discovery in going places. We have already seen a lot of this development in the marketplace, with benchmarking, "best practices," and common styling elements. As we saw in Chapter 2, it is not a new criticism. Many writers have complained about the loss of local specialties in foods and clothing, the disappearance of smaller outlets with idiosyncratic store owners, the impossibility of finding places that are unique and original, offering people and experiences that go beyond the mainstream. These complaints might seem quaint and old-fashioned to many, but one does not have to be a rank sentimentalist to take pride and pleasure in the variety that different countries' cultures offer.

One could argue in favor of globalization, pointing out that by and large, the globally successful brands and products are the "winners," incorporating the newest technology, the best designs, and the most reliable components. Overall, global products and brands show unrivaled quality-to-price ratios, the "best value for the money" kind of offering. Sure, some local products can still show higher quality, but that is usually because of a certain amount of artisan workmanship, handicraft skills that make the price exorbitant. Other local products are competitive only because of protection or some local monopoly.

But, local products are part of what renders the local culture different from that elsewhere. Local product offerings help define the people; they provide identity. As argued elsewhere in this book, when global brands try to take on the task of replacing this identity, they take on more than they legitimately should. They implicitly—and explicitly—suggest that what people had before is not worth as much as their offerings. The global marketers ignore the fact that it is the local culture, local products, and local brands that tell the people who they are.

Of course, the evidence so far is encouraging. As we have seen, countries have found ways of maintaining and even nurturing their local cultures underneath the globalization umbrella. The Internet is used to tie dispersed cultures together again, giving new hope to ethnic subgroups whose history has not been kind. Even the leaders of international organizations have recognized the need for supporting not only economic development, but also cultural rebirth.

It is the local idiosyncrasies that make people beautiful, not the homogeneous global brands. In one of the early demonstrations of what a computer could do, it was programmed to assemble a beautiful woman's face from the various "nicest features" input. Not surprisingly, the face was deemed ugly and virtually inhuman by all present. One hopes that the same adjectives won't be applied to the global marketplace of the future.

Index